265-Auditorium Theater Kansas

KANSAS CITY
Then & Now 2

Text and photos by
Monroe Dodd

★ KANSAS CITY STAR BOOKS

Book Design
Jean Donaldson Dodd

Dust jacket illustrations
Front: Quality Hill, north on Jefferson Street, about 1890, and the same scene in 2003 after construction of interstate highways through the area.
Back, in vertical pairs, from left: Main Street north from Missouri Avenue, top 1868, bottom 2003; Warner Plaza entrance on Main Street, top 1926, bottom 2003; Armour Road at Swift Avenue in North Kansas City, top 1962, bottom 2003.

Introduction photos
i: *Top, east on 11th Street from Main, 1940; bottom, east on Petticoat Lane from Main, 2003.*
ii-iii: *East on Ninth Street from Holmes, early 1900s.*
iii: *East on Ninth Street from Holmes, 2003.*
iv: *Top, Country Club Plaza, 2003.*
iv-v: *Country Club Plaza, 1930.*

Published by KANSAS CITY STAR BOOKS
1729 Grand Boulevard, Kansas City, Missouri 64108

First Edition

Library of Congress Card Number: 00-193004

ISBN 0-9740009-1-4

Printed in the United States of America
by Walsworth Publishing Co., Inc.
Marceline, Missouri

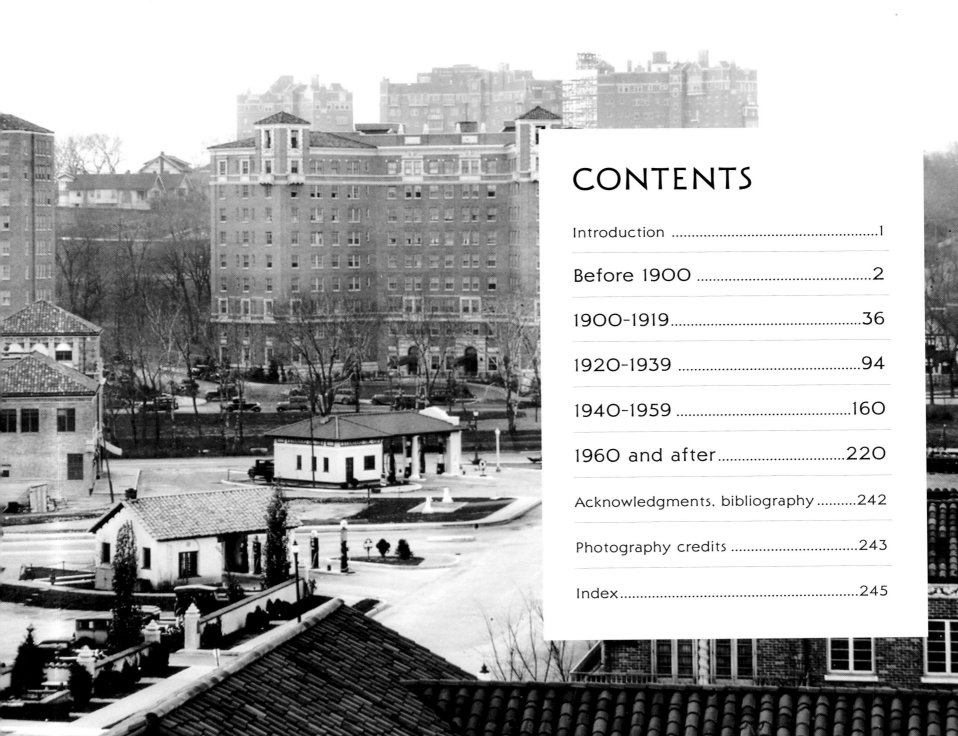

CONTENTS

Introduction 1

Before 1900 2

1900-1919..36

1920-1939 94

1940-1959 160

1960 and after..220

Acknowledgments, bibliography 242

Photography credits 243

Index..245

INTRODUCTION

Consider this book a passageway to the past.

You're about to see streets lined with hitching posts, or gas lamps, or Model T's. Fashions? You'll see ankle-length dresses and petticoats, jackets and bow ties and ever-present hats. A century ago, or decades ago, on those streets, Kansas Citians walked and worked and laughed and worried.

And you're about to see how those same streets look today. They are where *we* walk, work, laugh and worry. We wear different styles, but mostly we have the same kind of thoughts and passions as the people in the old pictures.

Connecting our present with our past — there's magic in it.

This is the second volume of photographs showing Kansas City then and Kansas City now. This book owes its existence to two happy facts: The first volume was well accepted, and sold out two printings. Second, Kansas City and its metropolitan area have a bounty of fascinating images captured over seven score decades. There were simply too many for a single book.

Like its predecessor, *Kansas City Then & Now*, this second volume shows downtown streetscapes, filled with long-departed storefronts and crowds of pedestrians. Additionally, *Kansas*

City Then & Now 2 samples the world beyond downtown Kansas City, scenes from Liberty and Little Blue, Olathe and Grain Valley, Lenexa and Excelsior Springs. The freeways that take us from one place to another, from home to work to shopping to entertainment, come in for extra attention in this volume. You'll see what things looked like before superhighways changed the way we see our city.

Often, the view of things then is more interesting, or more evocative, than the same view now. There are several reasons. Later architects sometimes were less capable than earlier ones. Old buildings were dangerous and had to be torn down. Renting out parking spaces on patches of asphalt paid better than renovating shaky structures.

And there's at least one more reason. *Then* pictures were framed according to the streetscape or landscape of the time, and according to the photographer's taste. *Now* pictures are framed strictly according to the *Then* picture. In each case, every effort was made to show what a photograph taken from the same spot would capture today.

If you occasionally find yourself ruing the loss of things past, keep in mind that old photographs cannot describe how things smelled, or how noisy things were, or how much pollution was in rivers or in the air that people breathed. Most surely, they cannot describe how people treated other people.

As with the first volume, this book doesn't try to judge which is better, past or present.

That's left to your judgment — and to your imagination.

— *Monroe Dodd*

Facing page: Herding sheep south on Pflumm Road, about 1910. From the Lenexa Historical Society.
Above: Pflumm Road, 2003.

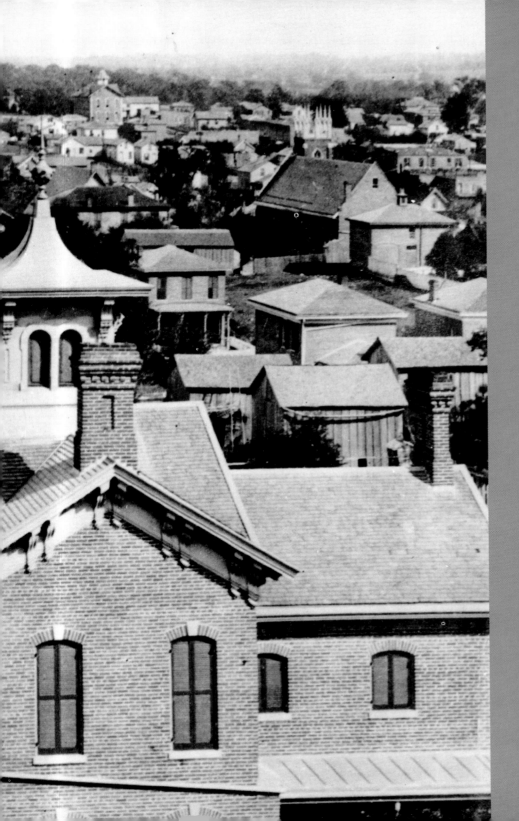

Before 1900

Investment in Kansas City boomed after 1866, when the railroads decided to build the first permanent bridge across the Missouri River here. A growing flock of land dealers and contractors placed their bets on the young city, and frontier-style wooden buildings gave way to brick structures. By 1868, as crews sank piers for the bridge into the sandy bottom of the river, stacks of bricks for new buildings sat on an unpaved Main Street. This view of the city's commercial hub is north from Missouri Avenue.

Today, a truncated Main Street extends north one block from the downtown freeway loop to Fifth Street, where it gives way to parking for the City Market. Left behind in the late 19th century as Kansas City commerce marched south, the City Market area now places its bets on renovated loft apartments and condominiums, offices for professionals and retail outlets.

Once-imposing earthen bluffs atop the south bank of the Missouri River gave way quickly to commercial development in the late 1860s and early 1870s. Mechanics' Bank, left, and Watkins Bank, right, occupied corners at Second and Main streets. The land topped by a farm fence to the east, across Main, would be carved away before the end of 1871. Construction would begin on a hotel there, but its developers would run out of money before it could open. In 1872, the Jackson County Court in Independence would buy the structure for a western branch of the courthouse.

Rail spurs and warehouses eventually dominated this area, which lies just north of the City Market. After 1915 the empire of philanthropist William Volker was based in the building on the right, which succeeded Watkins bank, and in an adjoining building facing Third Street. Volker grew wealthy making and distributing hardware and furnishings for the home, and he returned millions to Kansas City through bequests and charities. The structure on the left, which replaced Mechanics' Bank, today is occupied by a recycled-paper-products company.

Muddy, rutted streets and wood sidewalks connected the southern stretches of 1870s Kansas City. Tenth Street extended east in this view, which was from an upper-story window of the Coates House hotel. Most of these buildings were residences, interspersed with churches and some shops. A small peach orchard lay in the upper center of the photograph. By the 1880s homes and shops were giving way to multistory office buildings, and churches were moving to bigger structures farther south.

Office buildings and parking garages make canyons out of most of the streets today. Tenth Street has seen the coming and going of various financial institutions. The smallest building visible, on the northeast corner of 10th Street at Baltimore Avenue, left, was for decades home to First National Bank and its successors. It is being transformed into a new home for the Kansas City Public Library.

OLATHE
1872

Like other cities in the Kansas City region, Olathe joined the boom of the late 1860s and early 1870s. In 1868, Olathans built their first permanent school building, this stone structure at the northeast corner of Loula and Water streets. In the late 1870s, years before he became a world-renowned botanist, Missouri-born George Washington Carver would live nearby with Christopher and Lucy Seymour and attend this school. At first, the school held all grades; in 1882 Central elementary school would take younger students.

The old stone school building was replaced in 1898 with a new brick high school building. Today, John P. St. John High School on the northern part of this block has been converted into the Millcreek Center for technical education, with students from Olathe and other communities. It also is home to the Olathe Senior Center.

Developer, promoter, hotelier and farmer, Elijah Milton McGee cut a flamboyant swath in the Kansas City of the middle 1800s. McGee, a Kentucky native, arrived in the area in the late 1820s with his parents and 15 siblings. He wandered west, eventually to California, where he hit it rich in the gold rush of the late 1840s. Back in Kansas City, he purchased 160 acres on the outskirts of the settlement south of today's 12th Street. There he developed McGee's Addition. On the slope of a nearby hill, south of 16th Street, McGee built this farmhouse, compete with an entrance gate made of whale jawbones. Here he played host to various groups, which this day included a brass band.

McGee died in 1873 after one term as mayor of Kansas City. His house survived for several years, but streets were laid through his farm. Today, wide Baltimore Avenue splits the old McGee farmstead.

LIBERTY
1885

East side, West side: Liberty was established in 1822 as the seat of Clay County, incorporated as a town in 1829 and thrived well before the Civil War. The census-taker counted almost 1,500 residents in 1880, and when these photographs were made a few years later substantial business structures lined the Clay County courthouse square. On both sides, merchants hung memorial displays for the death of former president and Civil War hero Ulysses S. Grant.

On the east side of the square later buildings have replaced the 1885 structures. On the west side, the Clay County Historical Museum occupies a building that's little changed externally in more than 125 years. It contains re-creations of 19th-century rooms and displays of artifacts. The city of Liberty had a population of more than 26,000 in the 2000 census, and today it sprawls far from its original hub. Boosted by new subdivisions and businesses, Clay County grew by 20 percent in the decade of the 90s. The census counted more than 184,000 residents of the county.

NINTH STREET
1888

Another wave of investment swept through the American west in the 1880s, and Kansas City was a big beneficiary. New businesses and jobs drew tens of thousands of new residents, and that attracted people with ideas for moving those people from place to place. Engineer Robert Gillham devised a cable car system that connected Union Depot in the West Bottoms with the city atop the bluffs. After a thrilling — some said harrowing — ride up a steep trestle to Quality Hill, cable car passengers had this view of the young city as they rode east on Ninth Street. To their right was the powerhouse for the moving underground cable. On their left was the Thayer Building, designed by Chicago architect Walter Root and constructed in 1883.

The cable car tracks are long gone, and residences occupy the land where the cable powerhouse once stood. Yet in a much-changed urban landscape the Thayer building still stands, now connected with two adjacent buildings to its north. In the early 1980s their facades were preserved and interiors gutted to form a single complex called Thayer Place. The property changed hands several times after its renovation because of downtown's shifting demands for office space.

V-3156
PHOTOVIEW

For several decades in the 19th century the right neighborhood for prominent business owners and their families was the high ground atop the bluffs just west of downtown. It was called Quality Hill. Substantial — if not palatial — homes lined Washington, Pennsylvania and Jefferson streets from Eighth Street south for blocks. About 1890 the city began to bring its streets up to the standard of its buildings, not only downtown but also in residential areas. This view, which looked north toward Quality Hill from 14th Street, was captured to show off the new paving of Jefferson Street.

Earth-moving equipment dug up big chunks of the west bluffs in the 1960s, and Jefferson Street south of 13th ceased to exist. Interstate 35 now sweeps through the area, crossed by an access ramp from 13th Street to I-35's southbound lanes. A one-block section of Jefferson remains in this view, extending from 13th to 12th streets.

The man often acknowledged as the city's pioneer architect, Asa Beebe Cross, had his office on Missouri Avenue at left. Cross is credited with many of Kansas City's most imposing 19th-century structures, among them the Pacific House Hotel and the old Board of Trade Building on Delaware, Vaughan's Diamond building at the Junction of Ninth, Main and Delaware streets, and the old County Courthouse on Fifth Street. At the end of the block in this view to the east stood the Nelson Building, sometimes called the New Nelson Building, at Main Street. The stone-walled structure, originally popular with lawyers for their offices, was built in the economic boom of 1886.

All the buildings that once lined this block of Missouri Avenue, along with the block itself, have been removed. The north part of the freeway loop and its access streets replaced them in the 1950s. Now Independence Avenue extends into the scene from the east. The Nelson building, used after 1932 by the Helping Hand Institute and the City Union Mission, burned in 1952 before freeway construction could take it.

Acting on the discovery of a cold-water mineral spring at the Fishing River in 1880, developers began promoting and developing the resort town of Excelsior Springs. By the middle of the decade several springs with various amounts of minerals — each spring said to have curative powers — were being marketed to the public. In 1888, the Elms Hotel was constructed in a 1,000-acre park beside the Fishing River. The entrance faced east, toward a fountain and the river. Built of wood with broad verandas and paths to various springs, the Elms contained hot and cold baths for visitors. The hotel complex featured a swimming pool, bowling alley, target range and billiards room.

A decade after opening, the Elms burned in 1898. Ten years passed before a new, stone-walled Elms Hotel rose south of the first one. Within months it, too, burned. To raise money for a third incarnation of the Elms, the land where the first version stood was divided into these residential lots facing Elms Boulevard and sold.

One of Kansas City's smaller hotels was also one of its longest-lasting. The Virginia Hotel, which stood on the northwest corner of Washington and 11th streets on the western side of downtown, was designed by Kansas City architects Louis Curtiss and Frederick Gunn. It was the result of connecting and expanding two 1870s buildings on the site. The hotel's early managers, sisters Ella and Emma Garnett, oversaw a dining room that was popular among the city's prominent families.

The Virginia continued to operate as a hotel into the 1970s, but stood vacant until the early 1990s. Then, amid a rush of redevelopment on Quality Hill, the building and an adjacent structure were adopted for the headquarters of the Heart of America United Way.

Before the arrival of interurban rail lines after the turn of the century, horses were the quickest way to get around the countryside and into the city — particularly for residents of a town such as Shawnee, which the railroads bypassed. Here, two unidentified men showed off their team and buggy on the west side of City Park at the center of Shawnee. In the background to the east were the park bandstand and Archer's Store.

Only in the late 1950s, when the town passed 10,000 in population, did Shawnee build its own city hall. The site was the old City Park, chosen because it already was city property. As Shawnee boomed — adding a thousand residents a year through the 1980s and 1990s until by 2000 it had nearly 48,000 — the hall was enlarged to its current 30,000 square feet.

EIGHTH STREET TUNNEL
LATE 1800S

Bored into the side of Quality Hill in 1887, this tunnel carried passengers on cable cars and later electric streetcars to and from the West Bottoms. There, the streetcar line followed elevated tracks to Kansas City, Kansas. Seeking a safer route at a gentler grade after the turn of the century, the Metropolitan Street Railway would dig a new tunnel. The new route would begin at the same western portal as the old, but exit at a new opening on the east, which was near Broadway. This portal would be closed.

Streetcars made the last trip through the tunnel in 1956. In the 1990s this new structure arose as part of DST Systems' design for a revival of the northwest edge of downtown.

Underneath it lies the old tunnel, which was never filled in.

Built in the 1880s when Quality Hill was still the home of prominent Kansas Citians, the Washington Hotel was a fashionable residence. Mary Atkins, whose benefactions would help build the city's art gallery in the 1930s, was among those who lived in this hotel. The Washington had 132 rooms, most of them large and well-appointed. It stood at the southeast corner of Washington and 12th streets.

Kansas City Southern Industries Inc. opened its new downtown headquarters building here in 2002, almost half a century after the Washington Hotel burned and the site was cleared for parking.

KANSAS CITY ROAD
1899

In the 19th century, the small towns that surrounded Kansas City were themselves surrounded by farms. This acreage in Johnson County, Kansas, about 16 miles southwest of the city, was settled by German immigrants William and Margaretha Lackman in 1885. Within three years, the Lackmans had completed a grand farmhouse and outbuildings.

These two snapshots, taken in December 1899, showed a panorama of the Lackman farm as it appeared from the eastern side — from the barn with its windmill, facing page, to the house with its white wooden fence, above. The Lackman farm was three miles northeast of Olathe and four miles from the unincorporated community of Lenexa.

Financially battered by 1908, William Lackman sold his farm to Frank Thompson, whose family held the property until the middle 1980s. The Thompsons built the current barn in 1932 when the older structure burned. In the 1960s this property was annexed by the rapidly growing city of Lenexa.

In the 1990s, the home was refurbished and converted into the headquarters of the Lenexa Chamber of Commerce. The 1932 barn, facing page, was included in a state-of-the-art conference center, which opened in January 2003. The barn is in the Southlake Business Park.

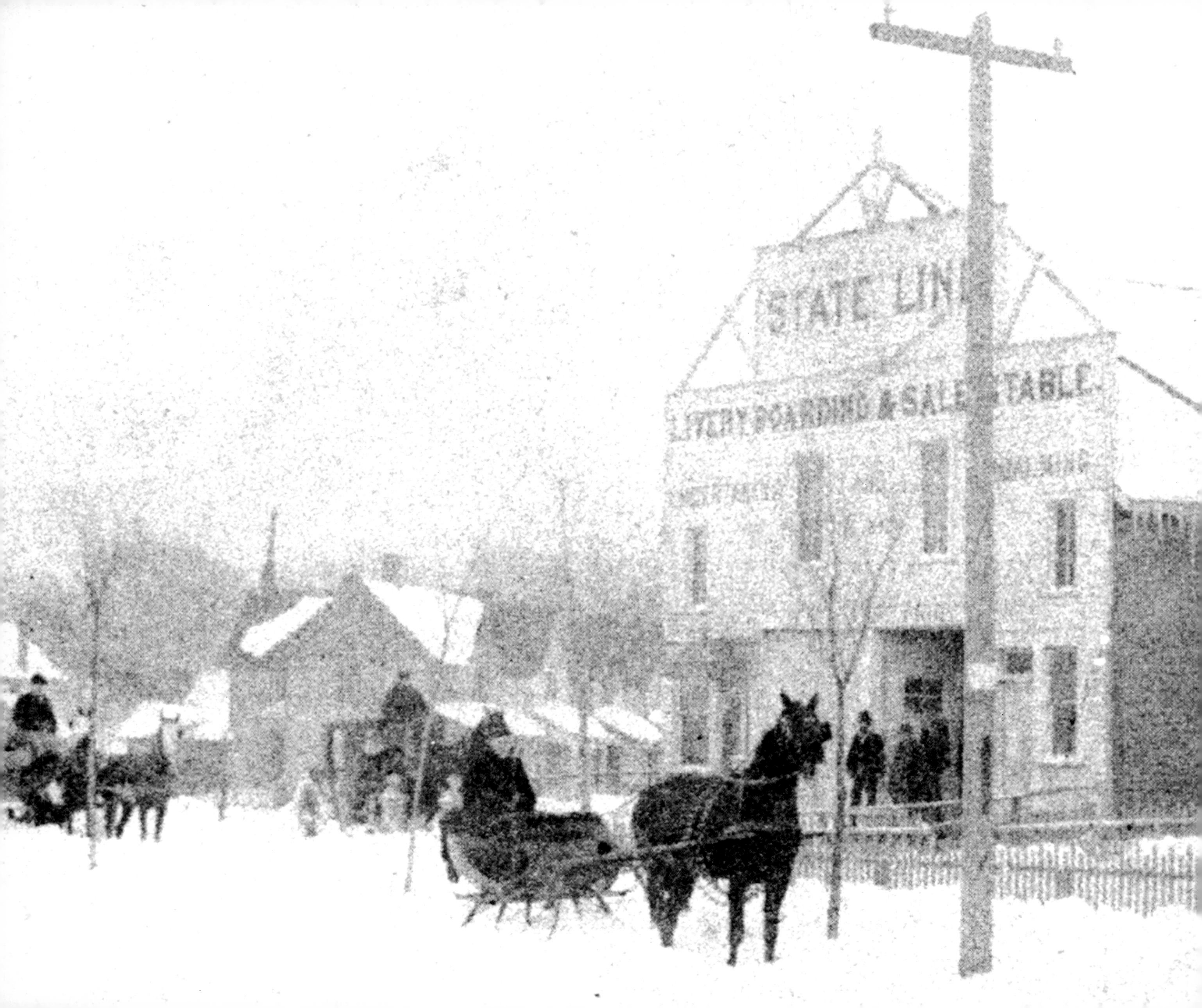
STATE LIN
LIVERY BOARDING & SALE STABLE

1900–
1919

Troost Park was created in the late 1880s in the area's first wave of amusement-park construction. Like Washington Park to the east and Chelsea Park to the west, Troost Park was developed by a streetcar company with the ultimate aim of not only entertaining patrons but also encouraging them to buy land nearby. The boathouse was one of the first structures at the park, which at its beginning stretched from 27th Street to Springfield Avenue, later renamed 31st Street. Atop the hill in the distance was the mansion built by I.M. Ridge, a Kansas City physician, in the early 1880s.

In 1902 Troost Park was turned over to the Kansas City parks department. Construction of the Paseo across it sharply reduced the park's acreage. In the late 1910s an arched concrete bridge was constructed to carry 27th Street over Vine Street at an easy grade. The Ridge mansion was demolished in 1930 and Lincoln High School — now Lincoln Academy — was built on the prominent site.

130—City Hall, Argentine, Kan.

From its founding in 1880 on the south bank of the Kansas River and for three decades afterward, Argentine was an independent city. Its main industries were rail yards and a smelter that drew silver, gold, lead and other metals out of ore shipped in from the west and southwest. This was the Argentine City Hall, constructed in 1891 on the southwest corner of Fourth Street and Silver Avenue. The jail was in the basement, the fire department on the first floor and council rooms on the second.

At the turn of the century, as new smelters were opened — many of them closer to the places that ores were mined — the Argentine smelter's work diminished rapidly. In 1901 it was closed, throwing hundreds out of work. In 1903, floodwaters from the Kansas River lapped into Armourdale, followed by lesser floods in 1904 and 1908. For these and other reasons the city struggled financially and began seeking to be annexed to Kansas City, Kansas. After several rebuffs, the 8,000 residents of Argentine were brought into Kansas City, Kansas, in 1910. Most of City Hall was demolished in 1930, and all of it disappeared by 1958, leaving this hillside to trees and brush.

The Shawnee Indian Mission, from the time of its founder's death in 1862 until it was purchased by the state in 1927, passed through various private hands. Although Westport was only two miles distant, the mission and the area around it remained steadfastly rural into the early 20th century. Mission Road was a country lane. The mission buildings numbered in the teens at its peak of pre-Civil War activity under the guidance of the Rev. Thomas Johnson, but as years passed only three brick structures survived. This was the north building, erected in 1845.

Undergoing one of its periodic refurbishments, the mission site is operated today by the Kansas State Historical Society. Various festivals staged through the year draw visitors to the buildings, which contain displays of how life was lived at the Indian trade school before the Civil War.

Remodeled and expanded two years before this photo was made, the home of William Waggoner and his family stood on spacious grounds across the street from the family flour mill and several blocks south of the courthouse square in Independence. With more than 20 rooms and eight fireplaces, the remodeling doubled the mansion's size from when artist George Caleb Bingham lived here in the late 1860s. It was Bingham, however, who made the property memorable. In the wood studio at right he was said to have painted two versions of "Order No. 11." That painting was Bingham's attempt to vilify the Union general whose Civil War order evicted many western Missourians from their homes. The artist bought this property in 1864 and sold it in 1870, moving to Kansas City.

Appearing much the same as it did a century before, the mansion is available for tours, historical programs, wedding receptions and other public uses. It was purchased in 1979 by the Bingham-Waggoner Historical Society, an Independence-based group formed to save the home. Bingham's wood studio was demolished decades ago by one of the Waggoner family owners and a carriage house was built in the area.

ROSEDALE
1903

Enough snow fell on this day a century ago to warrant the use of horse-drawn sleighs. This sleigh was traveling along Southwest Boulevard in front of State Line Livery, a well-regarded stable just west of the Kansas-Missouri line. The same year, Horatio and Mary Gates, owners of the stable, supplied horses and carriage for the Kansas City visit of President Theodore Roosevelt. The Gateses, like owners of some other stables of the time, combined undertaking with livery, and each served as an officer of the Kansas Embalmers' Board.

The Gates' stable burned in 1915 and was replaced with a "fireproof" establishment nearby. In 1922, the same year that the city of Rosedale was annexed by Kansas City, Kansas, the Gateses built a three-story funeral home at 41st Avenue and State Line. In 1980 that building was converted to the Ronald McDonald House for families of children receiving treatment for serious diseases. Today the Gates' old site on Southwest Boulevard is occupied by a convenience store.

A familiar pattern among Kansas City's pioneer church congregations was to begin with a small wood-frame structure near the center of town, then build a much grander church of brick or stone downtown, and then move south as residential areas sprang up in that direction. First Baptist Church, whose second home was here on the southwest corner of Baltimore and 12th Street, exemplified that pattern. Built in 1880, this brick structure with its tower was for more than three decades a landmark.

In 1915 the Muehlebach Hotel opened on the site, eventually becoming the city's best known lodging. The 500-room hotel was built by the Muehlebach Estate Co., under George E. Muehlebach, son of a pioneering Kansas City brewer. Presidents and former presidents from Theodore Roosevelt to Richard Nixon stayed here, the most frequent of them Harry S. Truman. As for First Baptist Church, by 1909 the congregation had outgrown the building and the 900 members moved to Linwood Boulevard at Park Street. Eventually, the church transplanted itself to 100 W. Red Bridge Road.

Wealthy cattleman C.C. Quinlan invested heavily in Kansas City real estate in the boom of the 1880s, and his Quinlan Place apartments exemplified the extravagance of some Victorian-era architecture. Turreted, onion-domed and ornate from roof to ground, Quinlan Place was one of several similar large apartment structures that sprang up across town. Towering over the northeast corner of Eighth Street and Highland, the structure was promoted as the biggest of its kind in Kansas City. Financial reverses eventually forced Quinlan to sell the structure in 1909 and it was renamed Walker Place after the new owner, J. Frank Walker.

Like most of its lavishly Victorian competitors such as the Garland Apartments and Tullis Place, Walker Place eventually was demolished. A one-story building occupies the site today.

265-Auditorium Theater Kansas City Mo.

Fires were common at Kansas City's early theaters, the Auditorium Theater among them. But unlike the Coates Opera House and some others, the Auditorium rose again. The first theater here at the northeast corner of Ninth and Holmes streets was the Warder Grand Opera House, one of the city's three leading theaters when it opened in 1887. With a change in ownership in 1890 came a change in name to the Auditorium. Fire devastated the building a few days before Christmas 1897 and it was rebuilt the next year. Still named the Auditorium, parts of two walls were reused. In its heyday, the Auditorium featured live presentations but in the late 1910s it would be converted to a movie house.

Part of the Auditorium was demolished in 1945, and in 1960 the rest burned to the ground. Today Holmes has been rerouted on a northwesterly angle north of Ninth Street and the area is covered by parking lots.

Ever the exponent of his church and of his city, pioneer Roman Catholic Father Bernard Donnelly persuaded the Redemptorist Fathers in the late 1870s to set up residence in the Kansas City area. In 1878 the towered brick chapel in the background and the structure adjoining it to the right were built on a 10-acre site on the main route between Kansas City and Westport. This was the Redemptorist monastery, where the public could worship on an upper floor of the chapel. As the number of Catholic families grew, a collection was begun in the late 1880s to build a new church. In 1895 the church in the foreground, Our Lady of Perpetual Hope, opened on this site just east of Broadway.

LINWOOD BOULEVARD
2003

In 1912, a new, stone-faced French Gothic church was dedicated facing Broadway, the Redemptorist Our Lady of Perpetual Hope that stands today. Its spires are barely visible at the far right of this photo. The older church and the original monastery and chapel were replaced in the 1920s by the Redemptorist school, which dominates this scene facing the current Linwood Boulevard. Linwood replaced Hunter Avenue as the name of this street in 1926.

The Centropolis Hotel was built in 1880, fronting Fifth Street on the northwest corner of its intersection with Grand. The grandiose name of the Centropolis came from one proposed for the city itself by an early town-booster, William Gilpin. The Centropolis was a popular dinner place for theatergoers at the Gillis House one block west. It was the first hotel in Kansas City with electric lights. The hotel's front was divided into two wings in 1900 to give all rooms a window to the outdoors.

A victim of the city's move in the early 20th century away from the City Market area, the Centropolis waned as a destination hotel in the 1920s and was torn down in 1941. Its site is now a parking lot for City Market patrons.

In the late 19th century, promoters built streetcar lines and amusement parks to lure potential land-buyers to their developments. The Heim brothers had a different idea — getting customers for their brewery. First they acquired the streetcar line, which ran from the City Market area to their plant in the East Bottoms. In 1899 the family constructed

Electric Park between Montgall and Chestnut, Nicholson and Rochester Avenues, complete with a beer garden featuring beer piped directly from the brewery. The park featured a roller coaster, gardens and a fountain, all extensively lighted by electricity for nighttime use. The view is to the east.

As the city spread southward, the Heims moved Electric Park to a larger area north of Brush Creek. That park lasted until it was destroyed by fires in 1925 and 1934. In 1950, the city condemned the first Electric Park property and made it a playground. Later Chestnut Trafficway was constructed through the middle of the property, slicing the city park in two and leaving this open area where the entrance to the amusement park once stood.

Joining other neighborhood boys in a sprint down their northeast Kansas City residential street was Frank Hagaman — evidently the hatless youth on the right — whose family moved to Kansas City in 1900. The Hagamans had come from Illinois, part of a wave of newcomers to the area in the first decade of the 20th century. In those 10 years, the combined population of the two Kansas Citys grew by almost 50 percent, totaling almost 350,000 by 1910. Hagaman's father found work as a clerk. The Hagamans later moved to Kansas, where Frank became a Johnson County lawyer, legislator and eventually lieutenant governor. For 41 days in 1950 and 1951 he was interim governor of Kansas.

Some houses are missing and some have been expanded in the century since Frank Hagaman and his pals dashed down the street, but the east side of the 300 block of Askew remains intact — physically and as a neighborhood of working families.

Begun in the late 1850s near the point where the trails to Santa Fe and Oregon divided, the Johnson County farming community of Gardner lay about 10 miles southwest of Olathe and about 25 miles from Kansas City. In the latter part of the 19th century and well into the 20th, Gardner remained a rural trading center of a few hundred residents. Horses were tied to hitching posts beside raised wooden sidewalks in this view, made on a snowy day.

GARDNER
2003

Metropolitan growth has reached Gardner. The New Century AirCenter lies on its outskirts, and new office structures and residential subdivisions are popping up. Home values have risen as much as 16 percent in recent years.

The Wyandotte County Courthouse opened in 1883 — three years before the modern Kansas City, Kansas, was created — and was beginning to show its age when this photograph was made two decades later. The city that surrounded this site, which was the northwest corner of Minnesota and Seventh Street, was in the midst of a 25 percent population increase that would bring it to almost 100,000 residents in 1910. In 1916 county voters would approve a bond issue for a new courthouse.

Blocked by legal questions, Wyandotte County did not finish a new courthouse until 1927, two blocks south of the old site. In the early 1930s the old courthouse was condemned and the land sold. In 1938 Montgomery Ward & Co. opened a department store in this new building. In 1971, the company left declining Minnesota Avenue for the new Indian Springs Shopping Center and the building was occupied by the Board of Public Utilities.

The second Elms Hotel opened in 1909 south of the original Elms after that structure was destroyed by fire. But this new hotel barely survived a year before fire ravaged it in autumn 1910. Some parts of the stone structure would survive and be incorporated in a third incarnation of the hotel on the same site.

In September 1912 the latest Elms — with more than 200 rooms — was opened. Among its notable guests was Harry S. Truman, who on election night 1948 sneaked away from the crowds outside his home in Independence and, accompanied by Secret Service agents, checked in here. Early returns confirmed what most analysts believed: Truman would lose to Thomas Dewey. Trumen went to bed, but was awakened about

4 a.m. when the radio reported that the vote count was swinging in Truman's favor. The agents drove the president to his headquarters at the Muehlebach Hotel in Kansas City. Truman won the election. As for the Elms, it survived a downturn in tourism after World War II, when the health benefits of mineral water came into question, and is open today after a renovation in the late 1990s.

OLATHE
1 9 0 9

A city of barely 3,400 people in the early 1900s, Olathe was the seat of a county numbering fewer than 20,000. Just after the start of the 20th century Olathe in many ways remained a country town outside the reach of Kansas City. Change was in the offing, however, and it was visible in the rails of the new Missouri & Kansas Interurban electric railway, the Strang Line. The interurban ran from State Line in Kansas City to Olathe, following Park Street to its terminal. On it, Olathe passengers could travel northeast to Lenexa, Overland Park, Rosedale and over Kansas City streetcar tracks all the way downtown.

OLATHE
2 0 0 3

Although the Strang Line stopped running in 1940, the paving of highways beginning in the 1920s and construction of superhighways later in the 20th century joined Olathe to Kansas City and to the suburbs of northeast Johnson County. Today, development runs unbroken into Olathe and beyond. The city contained more than 93,000 people in 2000 and Johnson County boasted a population of about 450,000.

LEAVENWORTH
1909

Since 1827 home to a U.S. army post, the Leavenworth area in 1884 was selected as a home for injured veterans, one of several branches of the National Home for Disabled Volunteer Soldiers. Beginning in 1885, buildings went up on this ridge overlooking the Missouri River. Most structures were made of stone, or of brick made on the site, which was on the south edge of town. Up to three thousand veterans could be accommodated. In 1901 Carrie Nation visited the home to protest the saloons that had been established in the vicinity.

LEAVENWORTH
2003

Soldiers' homes around the country were combined in 1930 with the Veterans Bureau under a new Veterans Administration. This home, renamed the Eisenhower Veterans Affairs Medical Center and grown to 38 buildings from the original 17, still serves veterans. Many of its buildings are unused, and some were scheduled for demolition until area preservationists got involved. They persuaded the VA to work with a private developer to renovate and lease many of the structures, thus saving them.

Just arrived by train, these sheep were herded by men and dogs south along a dusty Pflumm Road. Pens for delivery of sheep and other livestock stood just to the north, beside the St. Louis & San Francisco Railroad tracks through Lenexa.

Though platted and settled in 1869, the town was not incorporated until 1907. This photograph, from the Lenexa Historical Society, is believed to have been made by businessman Edwin A. Legler for his newspaper.

Today Pflumm Road is a prime thoroughfare for Lenexa and cities north and south. Some old farm homes still stand along it, among them the two-story house just left of center in the photograph on the facing page. It is barely visible behind the large trees that now mark the landscape in much of settled Johnson County. Don Bonjour Elementary school is just to the right of this scene.

A little more than a decade after Kansas City annexed the city of Westport, parks commissioners were laying plans to extend the boulevard system through the area. This street, previously named named Hamilton and Washington, formed a natural southern extension of Broadway, but it was named Mill Creek Parkway after the stream that ran nearby. Soon it would be widened, paved, and its sidewalks lined with trees to become an official part of the boulevard system.

BROADWAY
2003

In 1948 this section of Mill Creek Parkway between Westport road and 43rd Street was renamed Broadway. It forms an easy automobile connection between the Westport district in the background and the Country Club Plaza.

Twenty-four feet wide and 60 feet long, this building housed the first bank in William Strang's new Johnson County residential subdivisions that began with the word "Overland." Overland Park, Overland Hill, Overland Heights, Overland View and Overland Place all were situated near Strang's electric interurban rail line to Kansas City. All were on land that Strang boasted was higher than any in Kansas City, where residents could well recall flooding in 1903. Strang's home is in the background on the left. The Overland Park State Bank was organized in March 1910.

Saved from razing when the bank decided it needed bigger quarters in 1955, the building today is home to the Cosmopolitan Club, a service club. Overland Park State Bank built a new structure several blocks east on 80th Street at the southwest corner of its intersection with Metcalf Avenue. In 1993, when Kansas allowed out-of-state ownership of banks, Overland Park State was bought by United Missouri Bancshares Inc.

WEST TERRACE PARK
ABOUT 1910

Part of the grand plan for Kansas City's parks and boulevards, West Terrace Park overlooked the smoky West Bottoms, home to rail lines, roundhouses, stockyards, packing plants, grain elevators and baking companies. This overlook stood at the top of a long stone staircase leading to Kersey Coates Drive below. Construction of the overlook and drive in 1904 scoured the hillside of shanties that had stood there for years. The bridge in the background carried cable cars and pedestrians along 12th Street from the bottoms up to the bluffs until 1913.

In the 1960s, construction of I-35 scoured the hillside of not only Kersey Coates Drive but also most of the stone staircase leading up to this overlook, which still stands at the foot of 10th Street. In the background is the 12th Street Viaduct, which opened for motor and streetcar traffic in 1915. Beyond that stand Kemper Arena and the Interstate 670 viaduct.

ROCKHILL ROAD
ABOUT 1910

This double-arched limestone bridge over Brush Creek was built in 1900 by William Rockhill Nelson of *The Star.* Nelson also commissioned the winding road that crossed it. The road passed east of Nelson's Oak Hall estate grounds, through the neighborhood that Nelson was developing.

Louis Curtiss, the Kansas City architect to whom Nelson often turned for additions to his mansion, designed the bridge. A motor car and a horsedrawn carriage were heading uphill to the southwest.

After nine decades of use, the bridge was replaced in 1991 by this fenced bridge, one of the first projects in the city's five-year push to control floods and beautify the area along Brush Creek.

MCCLURE'S COURT
1910s

These one-story brick flats faced each other, 11 on each side, along the alley called McClure's Court between 19th and 20th streets and between Grand Avenue and McGee Street. A similar brick row also faced McGee. Among the city's more notorious slums, they were known as McClure flats. *The Kansas City Star's* new building, opened in 1911, towered over the scene to the north.

Today, a parking lot covers the entire block that once housed McClure flats. Only a sliver of *The Star* tower is visible behind the former bank building at center left.

The Voight Building stood on 80th Street, wedged between Foster Street and the Strang Line. It was one of the two largest business structures in the community of Overland Park. The other was the Conser building, in the left background. When this photograph was taken the Voight building housed a drugstore on the ground floor and a real estate office on the second.

As in downtown Kansas City, fire was a continual hazard in outlying areas. Despite the creation of a volunteer Overland Park fire department in 1919, every building except three burned at least once. The Voight building, which had already burned in 1910, burned again in 1927. This one-story structure replaced it. The Conser building, never the victim of a fire, still stands.

The former home of Temple B'nai Jehudah, by this time occupied by the Salvation Army, dominated the intersection of 11th and Oak Street, left, until the Southwestern Bell Telephone Co. began laying plans for a big skyscraper across the street. By 1919 the house, the machine shop and garage and other buildings on the right would be gone, replaced by the 14-story telephone building, bearing loads of detailed terra cotta. At the end of 11th Street to the west, where the street was called Petticoat Lane, was the John Taylor Dry Goods Co. store.

The telephone building, to which 14 more floors were added in 1929, was covered in stucco by its owner in the middle 1970s. The aim was to give the landmark structure a modern look. Where the temple building once stood, a new parking garage opened in 2003.

Landscape architects Hare & Hare designed Waterway Park to extend in staggered parcels from Grandview Boulevard almost half a mile north to Washington Boulevard. At north and south they planned lakes surrounded by trees and walking paths. In a small parcel in the middle, between Minnesota and State avenues, Waterway Drive and 11th Street, they placed this limestone-walled sunken garden, reached by steps. At the bottom was a lily pond with a small fountain.

Evidently because it had become a chore for the city to maintain, the sunken garden was filled in some time in the 1920s or 1930s. Today, the area is a parking lot. A small part of the original stone wall that formed the southeast corner of the garden remains visible at upper left.

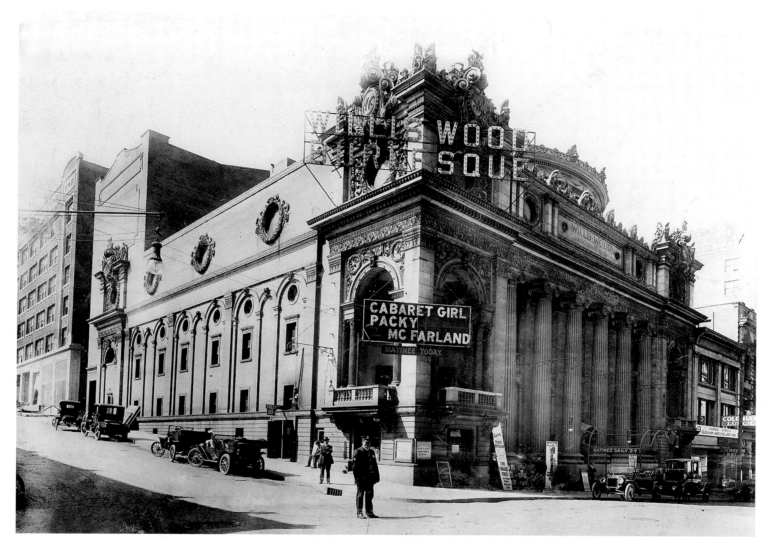

Past its prime as a first-class theater, the Willis Wood in late March 1914 was presenting the Cabaret Girls in a show described as "Interesting to worshippers of innocent frivolity." An added attraction was an appearance by Packy McFarland, a renowned lightweight boxer from 1904 to 1915. When the Willis Wood, named after its owner, opened in 1902 it was the ritziest in town. A tunnel connected the theater with the Baltimore Hotel across the street, easing the way for patrons to reach the hotel bar between acts. The Willis Wood's reign as the foremost theater in Kansas City began declining with the opening of the Shubert one block north in 1906.

In January 1917, not long after performers and stagehands had left for the night, the Willis Wood burned. In its place in the early 1920s rose the 22-story Kansas City Athletic Club building, occupied by the club in 1923. Most of this structure was turned into the Hotel Kansas Citian in 1933. It was remodeled five years later and renamed the Hotel Continental. After the hotel closed in 1982 the building was converted almost entirely to offices and named the Mark Twain Tower.

Flanked by boys and girls, and adults at a more discreet distance, doughboys marched east along Kansas Avenue from the square in Liberty. The United States was gearing up to enter the Great War in Europe and the country was brimming with patriotic fervor.

Liberty has preserved much of its courthouse square, including the buildings in the distance, which line the south side. Its new city building and its entrance plaza have taken the place of the steam laundry and other structures along this block of Kansas.

1920-1939

When Union Station opened in 1914, there was more to it than the massive passenger terminal on Pershing Road. The Kansas City Terminal Railway Co., the consortium of 12 railroads that built the station, also constructed this complex of roundhouse and yards about three-fourths of a mile southwest of the station. Here locomotives and cars were repaired, cleaned and stored. The land lay along Southwest Boulevard near 27th Street.

After years of neglect, the old rail yards have been converted into the Westside Business Park, which opened in 2002. Part of the old roundhouse was renovated for offices. The park was a joint effort by the Hispanic Economic Development Corp. and DST Realty, a commercial property developer.

The University of Kansas medical school moved into this imposing new building in 1924 when it opened Bell Memorial Hospital on Rainbow Boulevard at 39th Street in the Rosedale district. This building was named for Simeon B. Bell, a Rosedale physician and landowner who in the 1890s donated the land and buildings for the original medical school. That property, called Eleanor Taylor Bell Memorial hospital in memory of the doctor's wife, lay about a mile north and overlooked Southwest Boulevard. It would remain in use by the medical school until the early 1970s.

The medical school has expanded time and again. Bell's name was attached in 1979 to a new 850,000-square-foot diagnostic and treatment hospital on the now-sprawling grounds of the medical center. The former Bell building was renamed the Franklin D. Murphy Administrative Building after the former medical dean and later chancellor of the University of Kansas.

OAK STREET
MIDDLE 1920s

TROOST AVE.

BARSTOW SCHOOL

ROCKHILL ROAD

48TH

ST.

PIERCE AVE

ROCKHILL TENNIS CLUB

HOUSTON AVE

OAK STREET

47TH ST.

THE WILLIAM R. NELSON ESTATE
SOUTH OF BRUSH CREEK AND EAST OF OAK

Just north of Brush Creek, the land assembled by *The Kansas City Star's* founder, William Rockhill Nelson, began to change in the 1920s. The Sophian Plaza apartments, from which this photograph was made, opened in 1922 and the Barstow School's new home, upper right, in 1924. By 1927 the Whitehall apartments would rise at the southwest corner of Oak and Brush Creek Boulevard, lower right.

In the 1930s Menorah Hospital and the University of Kansas City opened on the hills south of Brush Creek. On the near side of the creek, the Rockhill Tennis Club moved out in the 1950s and the William Volker fountain was installed. By the early 1960s, a park called the cultural center mall took shape, named in 1966 for longtime parks commissioner Frank A. Theis. In 1999 Kauffman Legacy Park opened, far left. Menorah was replaced by the The Stowers Institute for Medical Research, which opened in 2000. Meanwhile, the street crossing Oak was renamed Emanuel Cleaver II Boulevard after the former mayor.

"The Shock Punch," a silent movie about a wealthy young man whose father wants to toughen him up, was playing at the Newman Theater when this photograph was taken in 1925. When the movie house opened six years earlier, it was Kansas City's most elegant. Italian tapestries hung from the walls, marble was used extensively on walls and floors, and there was a large chandelier and muraled dome. Next to the theater entrance was an outlet for Mrs. Stover's Bungalow candies, named for Clara Stover and the chocolates she made in her Denver bungalow. She moved to Kansas City with her husband, Russell Stover, named their company after him and turned it into a candymaking giant.

In 1947 the Newman became the Paramount. After a brief run in the late 1960s as a fourplex called the Towne, the building was razed in 1972 to make way for City Center Square.

Equipped with an innovative lift span to provide clearance for passing traffic on the river, the ASB bridge opened in late 1911 as a project of the Armour and Swift meatpacking interests and the Chicago, Burlington & Quincy railroad. It carried not only railroad traffic but also horsedrawn wagons, motor vehicles and electric railcars of the Kansas City, Clay County & St. Joseph. That interurban line, begun in 1913, split in North Kansas City, one route going north to St. Joseph and the other northeast to Excelsior Springs.

ASB BRIDGE
2003

The vehicle approaches to the ASB Bridge were closed and traffic moved to the new Heart of America bridge in 1987. The lower level still carries trains. In 1996 the remaining parts of the ASB were designated a national landmark in civil engineering. Bridge designer J.A.L. Waddell's memory was honored for his plan, which allowed the lower portion to be raised without disrupting traffic on the upper part. This and the 1920s photograph were taken from the Kansas City Cold Storage building, opened in the 1920s by the U.S. government to keep coast-to-coast produce shipments fresh.

For years one of the busiest arteries in Kansas City, this part of Troost was lined in the 1920s by one- and two-story buildings containing drugstores, markets and other small shops. Throughout this part of town, night clubs were opening where Kansas City's jazz reputation would be formed — particularly in the 1930s.

TROOST AVENUE
2003

A passenger bus terminal, the City Union Mission and other businesses in newer structures have changed the streetscape along this part of Troost.

WORNALL ROAD
1925

South of the Kansas City limits, Wornall Road descended this hill to a bridge over Indian Creek and continued south past the tiny community of Dallas before mounting the hills in the distance.

This area was annexed by the city in 1958 and now contains apartments, rest homes, restaurants and auto dealerships. Crossing the multilane Wornall in the distance is Interstate 435.

LENEXA
1 9 2 5

The Kansas City Road, giving motor vehicles the first all-paved route from Olathe to downtown Kansas City, was envisioned as an economic boon to the Johnson County towns along its route. One of those was Lenexa, where these bricks were being laid. The new highway stretched 18 miles from Olathe to Rosedale in Kansas City, Kansas. On Sept. 1, 1925, when the road was opened the full route, the first 13 miles from the south end were brick, three miles through Shawnee were temporarily macadam and the final two miles to Rosedale concrete. Grand opening ceremonies took place 12 days later in Olathe, featuring a bricklaying contest won by James Garfield "Indian Jim" Brown of the crew that built the highway.

The brick highway has long since been paved over. Today this portion through Lenexa is called Santa Fe Trail Drive. It was rerouted in 1990 to make way for additional parking in front of the businesses in the old town district.

This was a favorite place for musicians, artists and actors to have their studios, and many Kansas Citians in the early part of the 20th century took weekly music lessons here. The five-story buff brick structure was originally meant to house the Young Men's Christian Association. President Grover Cleveland and his wife laid the cornerstone for it in 1887. However, the YMCA ran out of money before the job was done. The contractor finished it and named it the Pepper building after himself. When the interior was ravaged by fire in 1907, it was refurbished and renamed the Studio Building.

The Studio Building was razed in 1972 for a parking lot. In 1998 the Charles Evans Whittaker U.S. Courthouse opened on the site, filling the entire block. With its crescent shape and massive glass walls, the Whittaker courthouse makes a far greater impression on the skyline than did the Studio Building. The courthouse was named for the only Kansas Citian, Missourian and native Kansan ever named to the U.S. Supreme Court.

A series of mostly two-story apartment buildings were built on either side of Warner Plaza in the 1920s with commercial space at the short street's entrance here at Main Street. The developers aimed to attract residents with a midtown location and a Spanish Mediterranean style. Warner Plaza was named for William Warner, on whose land the structures were built.

The neighborhood of Warner Plaza — its name loosely applied to several blocks north and south of the original street — eventually gained a reputation as a seedy, rundown area. In the 1990s, the neighborhood was cleared for a new shopping center, built with public aid in an attempt to revitalize midtown.

PERSHING ROAD
1927

Photographed one year after installation of the equestrian statue of George Washington, Washington Square Park was one of the newest arrivals in the parks and boulevard system. At right, the sign for the *Kansas City Journal-Post's* plant loomed behind the statue. At left was the 12-year-old Coca-Cola building with its distinguishing curved side, built to accommodate a rail spur.

The statue has been moved to a new spot in the park and most of the buildings that towered over Washington Park are gone, but the old Coca-Cola building is now being developed into loft apartments. Today it is called the Western Auto building, after the automobile parts company that began occupying space in the structure in 1928 and that bought it in 1951, topping it with a distinctive neon sign that remains there today.

Rolling westward through Wyandotte County over hilltop after hilltop was Victory Highway, which joined Parallel Avenue from the left, beyond the gasoline station in the foreground. Victory Highway, opened in 1921 and extending to San Francisco, honored Americans who lost their lives in the World War in 1917 and 1918. In 1926, U.S. highways received numbers in addition to names. U.S. 40 designated this route.

Now well within the boundaries of an expanded Kansas City, Kansas, this road is called Parallel Parkway. U.S. 40 has moved south. In a bow to the long-ago highway name, the road that converges with the parkway beyond this row of houses is called Victory Drive.

With close to 130,000 registered borrowers — almost double the number at the beginning of the 1920s — the Kansas City Public Library was feeling crowded in 1928 in its grand, stone-faced building at the northeast corner of Locust and Ninth streets. The building opened in 1897, meant to be a temple of learning and culture — and a symbol of Kansas City's maturity.

Since 1901 the second floor had housed the city's major public art gallery, the Western Gallery of Art. It contained copies of old masterpieces donated by William Rockhill Nelson, publisher of *The Star*. When the Nelson Gallery of Art opened a few years later near Brush Creek, the space crunch would be temporarily alleviated.

The public library departed this structure — then neither air-conditioned nor well-insulated — in 1960 for a modern, multistory building at 12th and McGee streets. For a while, this building held U.S. Trade Schools. In 1983, Ozark National Life moved its headquarters to the building and renovated it. Workers cleaned the marble and tile floors and leaded skylights, and they removed a dropped ceiling, discovering a hand-painted fresco underneath.

The San Dora Hotel building opened in 1926, renting street-level space to Weinberg Groceries, a laundry and a barber. These and other everyday one-and two-story buildings marked the neighborhood around 15th Street and Broadway on the southwest edge of downtown.

BROADWAY
2003

From the 1930s through the early 1960s, a string of groceries and other small establishments occupied space in the San Dora, later renamed the Stevens Hotel. In 1964 they disappeared as the way was cleared for construction of the south and western portions of the freeway loop. Today the neighborhood around the San Dora has been excavated for freeways and their access and exit ramps. This view looks west from the bridge next to the Bartle Hall extension.

A Kansas City fire and police station, this stone building at the southeast corner of Pennsylvania and 40th Terrace was built in 1897 to be the city hall of the then-separate city of Westport. According to the memory of a longtime Westport businessman, Albert Doerschuk, quoted in the late 1930s, the

Westport council met here only a few times before the city was absorbed by Kansas City in 1899. In fact, he recalled, the hall was rushed into being on purpose to use up the remaining money in the Westport treasury.

The turreted stone building survived until 1955, its last 10 years as offices of the Midwest Research Institute. A stone plaque bearing the names of Westport city officials of 1897 and of architect Frederick Hill was saved in the demolition and placed in the brick marker at the corner in 1959. In the mid-1980s, this building was built on the site and named Westport City Hall.

COUNTRY CLUB PLAZA
1930

Its southern edge marked by high-rise apartments that opened in the late 1920s, the Country Club Plaza continued to take shape in what had been pasture land in the valley of Brush Creek only a decade earlier. Atop the hill in the distance the Walnuts, soon to be the one of the area's most exclusive residential addresses, were being finished. Gasoline stations dotted Plaza streets and some construction was still under way, even at the outset of the Great Depression.

More apartment towers have risen on the south side of Brush Creek, while on the north side the Plaza has filled in with shops. No gasoline station now remains in the upscale shopping district.

Long past its prime, this mansard-roofed mansion at the southwest corner of Wyandotte and 16th streets once was the home of Prussian-born brewer Frank Hubbard Kump. Kump came to Kansas City in 1859, opening a factory that first made brooms and later ale and porter. He was first listed as a resident of this house in 1884, the same year he sold his successful brewery at 14th and Main streets to Ferdinand Heim of East St. Louis, Illinois. Heim and his brothers later opened a brewery in Kansas City's East Bottoms. Kump, who owned, rented and sold properties in the Kansas City area, lived here until 1897.

By the late 1910s, Kump's mansion had been converted into apartments. It was demolished by the mid-1930s, and the site has remained vacant since. Money is being raised to turn this hillside property and land west of it into a performing arts center with a landmark main structure overlooking the valley. Down the hill on Wyandotte the Webster School has been refurbished and its bell tower restored. The tower was part of the original design but was removed after a tornado in 1886 caused several deaths by toppling a similar tower at another school.

For years cars and trucks lined up on weekends at the farmers' market on the northeast corner of 38th Street and State Avenue. Here, customers could buy fresh fruits, vegetables and other commodities.

The Tower Plaza Shopping Center was constructed on the grounds of the old market in 1966, with a Sears store, Milgram's grocery and other shops. Today an Osco Drug has been built in the parking lot.

In the Johnson County countryside between the unincorporated community of Overland Park and the village of Stanley lay this stretch of U.S. 69, the major route to Fort Scott, Kansas. In the distance to the north, the graded road dipped to cross branches of Tomahawk Creek.

U.S. 69 and Metcalf Avenue have moved west, and this stretch just north of 135th Street is now called Old Metcalf Avenue. Although new buildings are popping up all around, and a shopping center is open just southeast of this scene, a 19th-century cemetery still tops the hill behind the retaining wall on the right.

WINNWOOD LAKE
ABOUT 1930

"The Atlantic City of the West"

Its shore covered with sand, Winnwood Lake — also called Winnwood Beach and Winnwood Park — drew thousands of swimmers and sunbathers to its site in rural Clay County beginning in the early 1910s. Winnwood's lake, formed by damming a small stream, eventually was lined with a bath house, dance pavilion, water slide and after 1928 by traditional features of an amusement park such as roller coasters. In 1913, the electric-powered interurban rail line north from Kansas City was built through the area, making it easily accessible from Kansas City, Liberty or Excelsior Springs.

From the late 1920s into the 1930s, Winnwood suffered fires, explosions and a collapse of its boardwalk that left 50 people injured. Eventually owner Frank Winn had to bow out, and the amusement park portion was closed. The swimming attraction continued in reduced form at the Lake until 1975. Today, the lake has been filled in and the area taken by a shopping center. A skating rink operates at left. Interstate 35 follows the route of the interurban across the area.

Designed as one big show window, the new home of the Boley Clothing Co. was built in 1909 at the northwest corner of Walnut and 12th Street. The glass-walled building was among the first of its kind in the United States and anticipated by several decades what became a common design for office structures. The Boley Building was designed by Kansas City architect Louis Curtiss. The Boley company itself lasted only until 1915. In 1931, Katz Drug Co. moved its headquarters here and installed on the ground floor what it called the largest drugstore in America. Real estate experts termed the corner the most valuable in Kansas City.

After a long succession of tenants, the Boley Building's exterior and its interior skeleton were preserved and renovated in the 1980s as part of the AT&T Town Pavilion complex. Nothing else remains of the 1931 streetscape along this part of Walnut.

MILL CREEK PARKWAY
1932

The Kansas City Public Service Co., the city's streetcar company, built this viaduct in 1927 to carry an electric-powered freight line from Westport across Mill Creek Parkway. Past the eastern end of the viaduct, the rails merged with the Country Club passenger route on the way to 85th Street and Prospect Avenue. The Chicago contractor worked with architect Edward Buehler Delk and the Municipal Art Commission to design the graceful, 310-foot bridge. It replaced a wooden trestle.

The Mill Creek viaduct was removed in 1996, three decades after it was last used by rail traffic. The Kansas City Area Transportation Authority, owner of the structure, deemed it unsafe for vehicle traffic and a playground for graffiti artists.

Other officials complained that it acted as a visual barrier between Westport and the Country Club Plaza. Mill Creek Parkway has been renamed Broadway to 43rd Street, center, and J.C. Nichols Parkway beyond that.

RESULTS OF COUNTY PLANNING

JACKSON COUNTY
MISSOURI

In 1933 the Jackson County Court, not a court of law but the name for the elected administrative body of the county, published a paperback album of scenes from various spots in the county. They were photographed by Dick Millard Sr. Entitled *Results of County Planning*, the court clearly wanted to show off its public works, most of them road paving. The next four scenes are from that volume, which evidently was distributed to other officials around the country accompanied by a letter on County Court stationery explaining the effort:

> "Jackson County, Missouri, at the crossroads of the nation, has a constant stream of travelers from every section. We have had good highways, to an extent, but not the modern system that came about after the adoption of a definite County Plan. That system is now complete....it has opened up new wonders, new beauty and new farm values as we had not in the beginning anticipated."

The letter was signed by the presiding judge, Harry S. Truman.

GRAIN VALLEY
1933

"...Located in Sni-A-Bar Valley on State Highway 40 and County Highway No. 20-E. The street scene...is the main thoroughfare." That was part of the description from the county's photo book. Grain Valley was a tiny farming center in the eastern part of the county.

Booming with new housing, Grain Valley's population doubled and more in the 1990s, surpassing 5,000 in the 2000 census. Like many small towns that experience rapid growth in the 20th century, much of the activity occurred away from downtown. The portion beyond the railroad crossing remains recognizable 50 years later.

HOLMES ROAD
1933

In the southwest corner of Jackson County, Holmes Road curved northward toward Martin City, where a few small buildings were visible.

Still a rural area, although annexed in Kansas City's outward march, Holmes Road now passes assorted sports training facilities, shops and restaurants on its way through Martin City.

Opened in 1908 as Patterson Hall on the Jackson County poor farm, this facility was renamed the Jackson County Home for the Aged and Infirm in 1911. An expansion bearing Presiding Judge Harry S. Truman's name on the cornerstone was opened in 1930. The County Court's 1933 book called it and the county hospital next door "institutions of kindliness," and pointed out that the county had invested $1.5 million in the complex. The view looks west.

Expansions have blocked the view of the older building, the grounds of which have been annexed by Kansas City. For years the facility was called Truman Medical Center East, a branch of the public hospital in downtown Kansas City. In 2001 it was renamed Truman Medical Center Lakewood, after the Lakewood Subdivision in nearby Lee's Summit. It sits at Gregory Boulevard and Lee's Summit Road. More expansions were announced in early 2003.

LITTLE BLUE
1933

Extolled as a "neighborly gathering place" in the County Court's 1933 book, residents of Little Blue had to flag down trains for transportation.

The tiny community was annexed by Kansas City in 1961, yet physically is little changed. It sits on Little Blue Road about a half-mile east of Noland Road, in an arm of the city that lies amid Raytown, Lee's Summit and Unity Village.

Coal, furnaces, stoves, wagons and watering cans — the Hunt stores sold a wide variety of hardware and home implements in the Westport area. The row of buildings clearly dated to the days before 1899, when Westport was an independent city.

The little stores and houses have long since disappeared. The heart of Westport has for decades been an entertainment and retail district.

LIBERTY
1935

Since 1859, two years before the Civil War, this courthouse had been the hub of Clay County legal activity. With plans for a modern new building in the works for the courthouse square, demolition was under way in March 1935. The statue on top, representing Justice, was coming down when this photo was made.

Decades after a Clay Countian paid a workman $10 for the wooden statue, it was handed over to a historic northland restaurant, Sandy's Oak Ridge Manor. There it stood until the 1980s when the restaurant owners gave it back to the county.

The statue has been renovated and placed in the Clay County Museum, across the street from the site of the courthouse that it once topped.

PENN VALLEY PARK
1935

This was part of the original 1893 plan for the Kansas City parks and boulevard system, but advocates of Penn Valley Park had to fend off turn-of-the-century critics who complained about the park's size and the necessity for it. the backers won, and by 1906 the park was taking shape. Over the next decade and a half it gained most of its outstanding features — the Scout statue, the Pioneer Mother sculpture and the Liberty Memorial. Penn Valley Drive, which topped the bank behind the lake, curved through the park much the way designer George Kessler laid it out. Embankments, pedestals and structures in the park were made of local stone to blend with natural outcroppings.

The park looks much the way it has for decades, but the downtown skyline has changed dramatically. One Kansas City Place and Town Pavilion have outstripped the Power and Light building as the tallest structures. City hall, opened in 1937, splits the area today between the Jackson County Courthouse on the right and the old Southwestern Bell building on its left. This view looks northeast from the hillside below the Scout statue.

Along the east side of Penn Valley Park stood a bevy of car and truck dealers and parts shops. Mixed in with them were a lithography firm adjoining the Hall Brothers greeting-card company. This view, southeast from the top of the Liberty Memorial tower, showed Main Street, and Grand Avenue merging with it. McGee Street and Gillham Road lay beyond. The large structures just below the horizon stood along Linwood Boulevard.

The auto dealers are gone and Hallmark, the descendant of Hall Brothers, has developed much of the property south of its Crown Center shops and hotel complex. In the foreground are the Santa Fe Place apartments building and its garage. At left is the new high-rise home of the Shook Hardy & Bacon law firm. Grand now meets Main Street farther south.

This was the brook that gave Brookside Boulevard its name, a tiny streamway that carried water north to Brush Creek — but usually only after substantial rains. The Crestwood Shops are at right, and the Country Club route of the streetcar system is on the left. The bridge carried 55th Street across the creek — and also marked the temporary end of a city construction project that enclosed the brook as a concrete-box sewer from 51st Street south to this point. Over the protests of some property owners, who had to pay an assessment for the construction if their property was drained by it, the city was about to begin enclosing this portion south to 59th Street.

Controversy over enclosing the brook is as little remembered today as the brook itself. More attention has been paid to the old streetcar right-of-way. It lay dormant from the late 1950s, when the last streetcars traveled the route, until 1997. Then the Kansas City Area Transportation Authority began constructing the 10-foot-wide, crushed limestone Trolley Track trail for walking, running and cycling.

1940–1959

From the early years of the 20th century, Kansas City's streetcars used this viaduct to ease the grade from Baltimore Avenue up over Delaware and Main streets to Walnut Street. At Main Street a canopied station had stairs to the sidewalk below.

Every structure in the area — not only the streetcar viaduct but also all the buildings around — vanished by the 1960s in the name of urban renewal. Streetcars last used the route in 1956. The viaduct was removed the same year.

This was the view along "Petticoat Lane," the stretch of 11th east from Main Street, just before World War II. The nickname had been associated informally with the block since the late 19th century, evidently because of the area's long tradition of women's retailers and women customers. On the corner at right was Harzfeld's Womens Wear; to the left was Virginia Dare, a clothing store. A block farther east was the Emery, Bird, Thayer department store.

PETTICOAT LANE
2003

In 1966 the Kansas City Council officially designated this block Petticoat Lane. In years that followed, however, the area lost most of the retailing business that helped give it that name.

Today no clothing retailers remain. The intersection is dominated by a skywalk connecting a parking garage on Main with the buildings on the opposite corners.

LIBERTY MEMORIAL
1941

In early May 1941, when this photo was made, the Liberty Memorial was a constant reminder for Kansas Citians of war — the World War that had ended 23 years before and the war then under way in Europe. In the north Atlantic, German U-boats were sinking Allied shipping. The Royal Air Force was bombing Berlin and other cities. In the United States, pro-British groups were trying to increase popular support for more aid to the United Kingdom. Within a few days of when this photo was made, the British ambassador to the United States, Lord Halifax, would arrive in Kansas City on a nationwide goodwill tour.

LIBERTY MEMORIAL
2003

The Liberty Memorial was closed for safety reasons in 1994. After extensive renovation of its deck and new construction beneath, the tower and exhibition halls on either side were reopened with ceremonies in late May 2002.

The United States entered World War II within months of the time Johnson County dedicated this land between Olathe and Gardner, Kansas, for an auxiliary airport. Moving quickly to establish training bases, the Navy bought the property and in October 1942 opened the Naval Air Station. In an age before jets made contrails common sights, the caption of this Navy photograph characterized them this way: "Only rarely are atmospheric conditions such that this vapor, resembling a Cirrus cloud, becomes distinct. Temperatures of zero or colder, with a very moist atmosphere, are necessary." In the sky at right was a biplane.

Operated by the military until 1970, the Naval Air Station was decommissioned and transferred in 1973 to Johnson County. It was named the Johnson County Industrial Airport and businesses began renting space in existing buildings. In 1994 the name was changed to New Century AirCenter in hopes of encouraging more business use.

Big changes were in store for this downtown block in the late 1940s. The John Taylor Dry Goods Co., left, had operated here for years, in a prominent position at the western end of Petticoat Lane. In 1947 R.H. Macy & Co. bought out John Taylor, gaining control not only of that store but also considerable property to the right or north of it. Macy's would fill much of this block with its new store, which opened a few years later.

Macy's stayed on this block until 1986, and then Dillard's occupied the location until 1989, when it closed, citing operating losses. The building came down in 1996 and was replaced by a parking garage.

Flanked by a corner shoe store, a clothing store and a cafe, the entrance to the Hotel Lyndon took patrons to the three-story, balconied structure in the back. For decades, the intersection of Troost Avenue and 31st Street was one of Kansas City's busiest, and with that in mind the Jones Store decided to move in. In autumn 1947 the company announced plans to raze these buildings and construct a "complete department store...with all the modern aspects of lighting, air conditioning, escalators and merchandise displays." This site was to be part of a big expansion program in which Jones also would open stores in outlying cities.

The 54,000-square-foot Jones branch opened in March 1949. A few years later, Jones halted its far-flung expansion plans to concentrate on the Kansas City area. The Troost store lasted until 1967, when Montgomery Ward & Co. took over the space. The building has since undergone a succession of occupants.

St. Joseph Hospital stood here, on the northwest corner of Linwood and Prospect Avenue, from the time the building opened in 1917. When St. Joseph was founded on Quality Hill by the Sisters of St. Joseph of Carondelet, in 1874, it was the city's first private hospital.

St. Joseph moved to a new complex at I-435 and State Line Road in 1977, and after a few years demolition crews began taking the old building down. When only a pile of rubble remained in 1982, film crews used the site to film a scene for the TV movie, "The Day After." The ruins represented destruction after a nuclear holocaust. In the late 1980s the Linwood Shopping Center was built on this and surrounding property.

The Huron Building opened in 1924, and at the time it was the tallest commercial building in Kansas. The 12-story structure, adjacent to the Huron Cemetery, was a project of the city's Elks Benevolent and Charitable Association, which wanted to rent out space to support the club on the top floors. The building, 150 feet tall, housed the offices of doctors, lawyers and others for decades.

The last tenants moved out of the Huron Building in 1987 and vagrants and scavengers moved in. By the early 1990s, bricks were falling through the roofs of buildings below, sheets of roofing and parts of cornice were coming off in the wind, and the owner was behind in his taxes. In 1997 the city took over the Huron and in 1999 the structure was demolished by plastic explosives.

In 1949, the freeway that would one day become Interstate 70 was only a plan, as was the Paseo Bridge. Grand Avenue, and McGee, Oak and Locust streets ran uninterrupted and at street level into the City Market and the surrounding Old Town area. Each of those streets angled slightly northwest at Independence Avenue, where they entered the grid of the original city. Nineteenth-century surveyors had aligned the older area with the Missouri River front, not strictly east and west. In 1949, cars jammed the relatively few surface parking lots and most blocks still were dominated by buildings small or large.

Far fewer buildings and far more parking spaces are visible today south of the river — with the obvious exception of the Charles Evans Whittaker U.S. Courthouse in the foreground.

North of the river, much of the land has filled up in the last half-century.

GRAND AVENUE
1949

Downtown's widest street carried streetcars, buses, cars and pedestrians past assorted storefronts north of 13th Street. This block alone contained eight clothing and uniform stores, two furniture stores, a jeweler, a pinball arcade, a cafe, a photographer, a music store, a florist and individual stores selling appliances, office equipment, paint and wallpaper, and typewriters.

GRAND BOULEVARD
2003

Today, half the west side of the block is filled with a parking garage. Retail outlets are a barbecue restaurant, tattoo parlor, copying and printing center, tax preparer, a wig and beauty store and an optical store. Also on the block are a bail bondsman and a labor pool. The portion of Grand from Crown Center north to the Missouri River was designated a boulevard in the early 1990s. The change meant that maintenance was turned over to the Parks and Recreation Department, and that upgraded sidewalks and more trees and shrubs would be required in the future — particularly as new construction took place.

In 1948 this two-room schoolhouse in the unincorporated South Park community of northern Johnson County held 44 black children. Walker Elementary had no indoor plumbing and was equipped with hand-me-down items from other schools. A new school, South Park Elementary, was going up in the neighborhood, one with indoor plumbing, separate teachers and classrooms for each grade and an auditorium. But in those days when larger districts in Kansas were allowed to maintain "separate but equal" schools, the tiny district in South Park restricted the new school to white children only. Encouraged by white allies and helped by the NAACP, Walker parents sued. In 1949 the Kansas Supreme Court ruled that the black children must be allowed to attend the new, previously all-white school.

PHILADELPHIA BAPTIS
CHURCH
SUNDAY SCHOOL 10:0
MORNING WORSHIP 11:1
WEDNESDAY SERVICE
REV. J.-G. FLEMING P

The South Park neighborhood is now part of Merriam, and the former school building on West 50th Terrace has been modified considerably. It is now home to the Philadelphia Baptist Church. A plaque in a nearby park commemorates the late 1940s campaign to allow the black schoolchildren to attend the new school.

Vacant for eight years when this photograph was made, the old Kansas City Junior College building remained a sentimental landmark downtown. Not only junior college students but also earlier high school students recalled classes in the structure, which had been Central High School until 1915. After a brief period as the Polytechnic Institute, this was the Junior College until the 1940s, when classes were moved to 3845 McGee Street. In the 19th century various school buildings and additions had occupied this site at the southeast corner of 11th and Locust Street. The towered structure in the center of this picture was built in 1894; a wing to the south in 1884.

The old Junior College building, its tower and unused observatory standing until the end, was razed in 1953. For 20 years, this site was a parking lot. In the early 1970s, a new Kansas City Municipal Courts structure opened here.

The Last Chance was fabled as the tavern and gambling hall that straddled the Missouri-Kansas line. Authorities often accused its operators of shifting liquor bars, dice games, horse books and slot machines back and forth across the border inside these buildings to avoid prosecution. When one jurisdiction conducted a raid, according to prosecutors, offending items would be shoved into the other jurisdiction. Based on atlases and a special survey made for prosecutors, the state line entered the structures about where the covered doorway stood. Confusing matters, the line entered at an angle. The buildings stood on the southeast side of Southwest Boulevard, which runs northeast and southwest.

In April 1950 the Last Chance operation came under tight scrutiny after police learned it was the last place visited by reputed mobsters Charles Binaggio and Charles Gargotta before they were gunned down at their First Democratic Club on 15th Street. Those slayings contributed to a national outcry against mob activity and sparked a clampdown on liquor and gambling operations in the Kansas City area. The Last Chance building was destroyed by water and fire in the 1951 flood. Since then, 31st Street has been routed through the area and a restaurant built on what remains of the site.

Foreshadowing big changes in Kansas Citians' lives over the next decades, the Southwest Trafficway viaduct was under construction on the city's west side. At this stage, its supports looked much like a line of hurdles. Formally opened in November 1950, the viaduct portion of the longer Southwest Trafficway was the city's first multilane, limited-access route.

City planners intended for it to be joined by a highway ring into, out of and around downtown that would ease traffic congestion. When finished, the viaduct would begin just north of 26th and Summit streets, carry cars over the Terminal Railway tracks and Southwest Boulevard, and empty onto 10th Street at Washington Street.

Half a century old and having been repaired and expanded several times, the viaduct has long been joined to the U.S. Interstate highway system, which was devised in the 1950s. With Interstates 70 and 670, Interstate 35 carries people not only into and out of downtown, but also through the city, much more quickly than the pre-1950 street system. I-35 and other interstate routes through the heart of town also have been criticized for breaking up commercial districts and disrupting residential neighborhoods.

DOWNTOWN
1950

This half-century-old view to the north from atop the Liberty Memorial contains elements easily recognizable today. Union Station looked much the way it does now. In the distance, the Kansas City Power & Light building and other tall buildings stood as they still do. Yet on either side of Union Station were vast train sheds and sidings still in heavy use for carrying passengers to other cities and across the country. A streetcar was turning at Pershing Road and Main Street, lower right.

Today the train sheds are gone, and passenger trains are few. The sidings have been replaced by an office structure on the east and a science museum on the west. Skyscrapers built in the 1980s jam the skyline, diminishing the prominence of the Power & Light building, the Fidelity Bank building, and City Hall and the Jackson County Courthouse. Streetcars disappeared more than four decades ago. Union Station, having suffered years of neglect, was renovated in the 1990s into a tourist destination.

By the middle of the 20th century this part of town was in general decline. Here Main Street crossed Seventh and continued north into the City Market. Although somewhat picturesque, many of these buildings were in poor repair.

Together, the building of the north part of the freeway loop in the 1950s and urban renewal efforts extending into the 1960s cleared this part of downtown of most of its structures.

The older buildings in the center distance, opposite the freeway and near the City Market, still stand — unlike any of the structures on the near side of the freeway.

When the Wish-Bone restaurant opened in November 1949 at the northeast corner of Main and 45th streets, a plate dinner of fried chicken cost $1.75 and a family style dinner $2.25. Prime rib cost $2.75. The biggest customer buzz, though, was over the salad dressing — made from a recipe brought from Sicily by Lena Sollomi, mother of owner Phil Sollomi. Within a year, the dressing was being marketed to local stores and in 1952 Sollomi sold the restaurant to concentrate on manufacturing his Wish-Bone Salad Dressing for national distribution. In 1957 the operation was sold to Thomas J. Lipton Co., which built a plant in Independence, where Wish-Bone dressing still is made.

The Wish-Bone continued in operation as a family-style restaurant until 1978, when the turn-of-the-century building, originally a lumber magnate's home, was remodeled and converted into an upscale restaurant. That incarnation lasted only a few years. In 1982, a St. Louis firm began planning to remove the restaurant and construct an office and hotel development in its place. Today, the Kansas City Marriott Country Club Plaza hotel occupies the site.

Holstein dairy cattle rested in a field south of the Ralph E. Walters farm home in unincorporated Johnson County. The farm lay south of 95th Street and east of the two-laned Quivira.

Developers announced plans in 1970 for a big new retail mall on the acreage southeast of 95th and Quivira, and in 1975 the first stores opened in the Oak Park Shopping Center. It covered 1.34 million square feet then, and has since been enlarged. This scene looks north from near the southwest corner of the center's property.

By the middle of the 20th century, the south end of Quality Hill was receiving little attention. Grace and Holy Trinity Cathedral, out of view to the right of this picture, was the biggest activity in the neighborhood. Vacant lots like the one at left began to appear. Far more was taking place on the other side of Broadway, closer to the Municipal Auditorium, the Kansas City Club and the Aladdin and several other hotels near the Auditorium Garage. This view is east from Washington Street.

Bartle Hall straddles today's 13th Street like a leviathan. It blocks most of the former Aladdin, and One Kansas City Place and other newer skyscrapers have risen far above the pyramidal roof of the hotel, which is now the Holiday Inn Downtown Convention Center. At left, the east side of Washington Street between 13th and 12th now holds the Kansas City Southern Industries building.

Still almost a decade away from incorporation as a city, Overland Park showed the trappings of a small Kansas town — one- and two-story shops, gasoline station and bus terminal.

All were visible in this view north to where Santa Fe and Foster Street converged at 80th Street.

With almost 150,000 residents counted in the 2000 census, Overland Park has surpassed Kansas City, Kansas, as the largest city on the Kansas side of the metropolitan area. The city's growth in the 1990s exceeded even optimistic projections. As with many newer cities, however, that change is little in evidence in the old downtown area. Businesses have changed, but buildings and streets and water tower and power lines form much the same skyline as they did a half-century before. A notable difference is the Clock Tower, near the new Overland Park Farmer's Market at right.

Brand new, these highways carried motorists past the northeast edge of downtown and over the Missouri River by way of the recently opened Paseo toll bridge, to the right in this scene. In the distance, the divided highway would in a few years form the north part of the downtown freeway loop. These roads were part of the city's plan for a ring of limited-access routes to and from downtown. Eventually this route would join the Interstate highway system.

Following approximately the same path to and from the Paseo Bridge, the interstate highway in the distance curves under an array of overpasses to take motorists west to Kansas or south around the freeway loop.

SEPTEMBER 9, 1955

Going up: KCMO built its new, freestanding television tower next to its studios on 31st at Grand Avenue. The structure rose more than 1,400 feet from the ground, triple the height of the station's earlier tower. The station — one of several that went on the air in Kansas City shortly after the Federal Communications Commission in 1953 lifted its freeze on new licenses — was aiming to send a stronger signal. The first transmission from the new tower was made February 23, 1956, and the CBS affiliate eventually began promoting it as the "Eye-full tower" — with a nod not only to the Eiffel Tower in Paris, but also to the CBS logo.

When KCMO moved to Fairway in 1977, it provoked protests from politicians and community activists — and pleas from residents and business owners nearby to take its tower with it. They complained that falling ice and bolts were a hazard to those below. Nevertheless, the tower stayed and the station, which changed its initials to KCTV in 1983, continues to beam its signal to this tower for broadcast. KCPT, the area's public television station, moved into KCMO's old studios next door.

BROADWAY BRIDGE
1956

For more than two decades, the shortest auto route from downtown to the Municipal Airport was by way of a two-lane road above the railroad tracks on the Hannibal Bridge. Yet the trip could be frustrating if traffic was backed up or if the draw span of the bridge was open for traffic on the Missouri River. In late 1954, the city work began on a new bridge to carry Broadway across the river, high enough above the water for river craft to pass under safely. No longer would motorists have to wait for the draw span to close. The catch was that they would have to pay a toll. This view looks south from the north bank of the river. On September 5, 1956, the bridge opened. The toll was a dime for a trip to the airport and 15 cents to go all the way to U.S. 71.

BROADWAY BRIDGE

2003

At the end of 1990, the bridge toll — which had risen to a quarter — was dropped and the toll booths removed. The tolls had generated more than $40 million for the city coffers since the bridge opened, but were unpopular, particularly with northland residents and business leaders. In 1992 Kansas City handed control of the bridge over to the Missouri Department of Transportation.

Anticipating new business downtown because of the city's various annexations, the Jones Store in 1954 announced an overhaul at its main location, which occupied most of the block from 12th to 13th streets, Main to Walnut. The effort took four years. The store rebuilt seven buildings into which it extended, and remodeled two more, adding a street-level surface of red marble, above which was a sheathing of porcelain on steel. Through all the work, the Jones Store remained open.

By the mid-1990s the Jones Store was the last of the old-line department store retailers remaining downtown. In December 1997, saying that the store was losing money because of maintenance costs, the parent company of Jones Store announced the location would close. Its last shopping days were in January 1998.

As the so-called Grand Central Station of Waldo, this building was a place for Kansas Citians who lived near 75th Street and Wornall Road to catch the streetcar downtown, or for others to transfer to and from the streetcar that ran south and southeast to 85th Street and Prospect Avenue. When the

Waldo station was built in 1907, electric-powered streetcars replaced cars hauled by small steam engines on this route, and part of the station housed an electric generator. Another part held a restaurant.

The last stop by a scheduled streetcar in Kansas City occurred here after midnight on June 23, 1957. Right away, the old station was viewed as a waste of space, and in March 1958 it was demolished and a parking lot built in its place. At some places in the lot, the old streetcar tracks remain visible.

Trans World Airlines, then headquartered in Kansas City and the city's largest employer, consolidated its accounting, secretarial, sales and public relations offices in this building at the northwest corner of 18th and Main Street in late 1956. Atop the far corner, overlooking the intersection of 18th and Baltimore Avenue, was a floodlighted 35-foot "rocket ship." Airline publicity described it as "patterned after the famous TWA rocket at Disneyland" and called the icon "significant of TWA's role in aviation and a future replete with startling advances." The 1950s modern look was a radical departure from the building it replaced, the Muehlebach Brewery, right.

18TH STREET

Four years after the airline moved in, a sagging floor and other structural problems spurred a million-dollar revamping and remodeling. In the early 1970s, with the transfer of some TWA operations to the new Kansas City International Airport and more to cities in the East, TWA left and the building was leased by the U.S. government to house Social Security Administration offices. Today, TWA has been absorbed by another airline and this building stands vacant.

When it opened the year before, the Sixth Street Expressway — or freeway or trafficway, depending on who was describing it — represented Kansas City's first east-west, limited-access route. On the east, it connected with the Paseo Bridge and, via a cloverleaf intersection, with the ASB bridge. On the west, it flowed into the Intercity Viaduct, which extended westward in this view from the overpass that carried Broadway over the highway.

On-ramps and off-ramps have multiplied over the years to link this expressway with Interstate 35, forming the northwest portion of the freeway loop around downtown Kansas City.

Named Interstate 70 since the cross-country freeway was linked to this route, the road has seen several ramps to downtown closed or restricted to enhance safety or diminish congestion.

In 1949, seven years after the first drive-in theater in the Kansas City area opened on U.S. 40 in Jackson County, the number of outdoor movie shows had grown to five, and the newest was this one on Kansas Highway 10 in a rural part of Johnson County. In this week in early July 1958 the Shawnee was showing 'Bullwhip," starring Guy Madison and Rhonda Fleming. Their characters were billed as "Cold-blooded saddle tramp and hot-blooded hellcat!" The late fare at 11:30 p.m. was "Hot Rod Rumble," a tale of "Speed crazed teen-agers."

Attendance at Kansas City area drive-in theaters peaked in 1971, and as the metropolitan area spread outward the land they sat on often became more profitable to sell. The Shawnee Drive-In closed in spring 1979, a little more than a year after its sister drive-in, the Leawood on State Line Road. In the middle 1990s, the land where the drive-in sat was used for an expansion by Bayer Corp.'s Agriculture Division.

95TH STREET
LATE 1950S

Looking much like a country lane, 95th Street curved westward just past its intersection with Metcalf. A fishing pond and the Manor Barn restaurant lay just north of the road.

OVERLAND PARK

Now a multilaned nexus of Johnson County traffic, the intersection of 95th and Metcalf has for years been one of the busiest in the county. The pond is now a reflecting pool for twin glass-walled office buildings that stand just to the right of this scene at the northwest corner of the intersection. The other corners contain shopping centers.

1960
and
after

This building at the northeast corner of Grand and 12th Street was about to be razed, so merchants in early 1960 busied themselves selling stock and fixtures and posting "moved" signs. This two-story structure would give way to the multimillion-dollar, 20-story Traders Bank building, hailed as the first skyscraper built in Kansas City in a quarter-century.

Indeed, the last one was City Hall, which opened in 1937. The Traders building would open in summer 1962 with Traders National Bank on the bottom floors and rental offices on the floors above. Traders also was the first of a wave of glass-wall buildings that would rise in the city in years to come.

Almost four decades after it was built, this highrise was remodeled in 1999 and labeled Traders on Grand. The bank for which it was named, like many Kansas City banks in the late 20th century, changed hands many times. In 1984, Traders Bank was merged into Kansas City Bank & Trust Co., and renamed the Bank of Kansas City. Two years later, amid financial difficulties, the Bank of Kansas City was taken over by Merchants Bank. In the early 1990s Boatmen's First National took over Merchants, in 1997 NationsBank took over Boatmen's, and in 1998 NationsBank became part of Bank of America.

On the eve of the city's 50th anniversary, North Kansas City boosters characterized their retail district along Armour Road as retaining "a small-town friendliness in the shadow of Kansas City's skyscrapers." North Kansas City was conceived in the late 19th century. However, not until levees were built to keep out floodwaters and the Armour, Swift and Burlington bridge was constructed to carry traffic across the Missouri River was the North Kansas City Development Co. able to incorporate the village. That happened in November 1912. In 1962, these pedestrians were crossing Armour in the heart of the business area, at Swift Avenue.

Although much has changed around it, this remains an important retail intersection in North Kansas City. A long effort to attract commercial enterprise has brought more than 1,000 businesses to the city. The 4,700 people counted in the 2000 census represented the city's first population increase in decades.

12TH STREET
1965

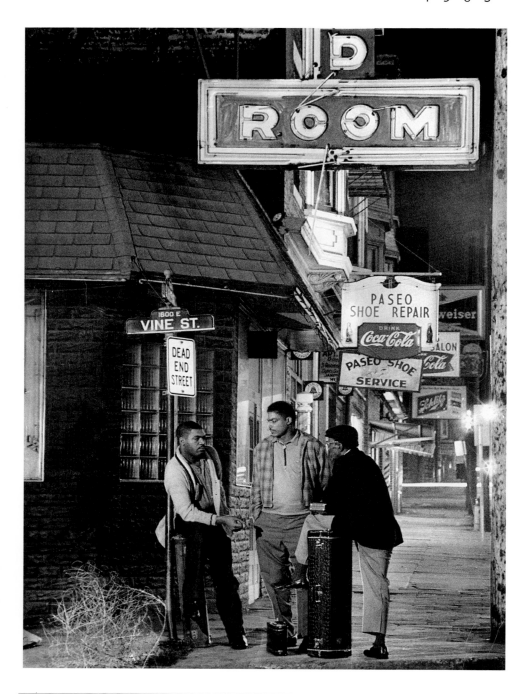

In the heyday of Kansas City jazz, dance halls and taverns stretched along 12th Street from Wyandotte to Cherry, past Troost, on to Vine Street and beyond. Twelfth and Vine occupied a hallowed place in jazz lore — in part because of the song, "Kansas City," which tells of "Standing on a corner, 12th Street and Vine...," but also because of the Orchid Room here at the southwest corner of 12th and Vine and other clubs in the area. Longtime residents recalled that the 12th and Vine nightclub scene, which peaked in the 1930s, carried on into the 1950s. By 1965, when this photo was taken to accompany a *Kansas City Star* article about the area, the Orchid Room was closed and the jazz scene in serious decline. Musicians Eddie Saunders, left, and Abdul Hameed, right, talked with Jimmy Smith.

12TH STREET

The Orchid Room and all the storefronts along 12th Street from Vine west to the Paseo have been removed, along with the intersection sign. Today the sign stands on the north side of 12th Street. Most of these blocks east of Paseo have been converted into parks or public housing. Much of the effort to revive the jazz scene has taken place six blocks south at 18th and Vine streets, historical hub of the black business community.

Four decades after the Country Club Plaza was begun, a half-size replica of the Giralda Tower in the southern Spanish city of Seville rose to mark the corner of the new Swanson's store. Developer J.C. Nichols had visited Seville in the 1920s, and been taken by its Giralda Tower, a 12th-century Moorish project topped by a 16th-century Christian belfry and a statue representing faith, called the *giraldillo*. As early as 1929, Nichols tried to incorporate the tower into a Plaza project, but never succeeded. Nichols' son and associates visited Seville in 1966, the same year Kansas City and Seville proclaimed themselves sister cities. They saw the 250-foot tower and decided to use a replica for the new Swanson's building.

In October 1967, a month after Swanson's opened, the 130-foot tall Giralda Tower replica was finished. For its opening ceremony, the tower was lit with a switch thrown by Mayor Felix Morena de la Cova of Seville, who headed a 44-member delegation from the Spanish city. Today the corner occupied by Swanson's is shared by a clothing store and a restaurant.

Over the decades, the Barry General store gained the reputation of being the oldest continuously operated store west of the Mississippi. True or not, a store was said to have operated on this Platte County site — just west of the Clay County line — as early as 1827. That would have put it in Indian Territory until the Platte Purchase annexed to Missouri the land that stretches west to the Missouri River. In 1837 this officially became Platte County. The store was part of the small community of Barry, which at its peak had two blacksmith shops, three churches and three other stores. The area was annexed by Kansas City, but when this picture was made farmers still dropped in on Saturdays to buy feed and hay.

By the 1980s, the store had been turned into a flea market with booths selling antiques, collectibles and miscellaneous items. Barry Road — a hilly, two-laned route long considered dangerous for motorists — finally was widened, and that required removal of the store. Also widened — and renamed — was the north-south road along the Platte and Clay county line. Formerly Baughman Road, it is now the Platte Purchase Parkway.

Using a converted girls' dormitory on the campus of the defunct Western University, Douglass Hospital moved to this site in 1945. It sat on a hill in the Quindaro area, overlooking the Kansas River bottoms. The address of the 50-bed hospital was 3700 N. 27th St. The institution, overseen by the African Methodist Episcopal Church, had seen several previous homes since its inception in 1898, most recently a 15-room former residence on Quindaro Boulevard. By the early 1960s the hospital, frequently strapped for money, saw its patronage decline to about half its capacity after larger white hospitals began to desegregate.

Douglass Hospital closed in summer 1978. The building, since razed, was the last remaining one of the old Western University, which was said to have been the first college-level school for black people west of the Mississippi River.

Rural Kansas or soon-to-be-developed Johnson County? It's the latter, with a one-lane bridge marked "Weight Limit 5 Tons." This was the scene on Nall Avenue, looking north past its intersection with 151st Street. As late as 1992, deadly traffic accidents brought complaints that this junction ought to have at least four-way stop signs, a 45-mph speed limit and lights of some kind.

Lighted, four-lane roads with passing lanes and stoplights form the junction of Nall and 151st Street today, the signs of the onrush of development. Houses are visible atop the horizon and plans are being made for construction of an office and retail center on the southeast corner. Nall forms the boundary between Overland Park on the west and Leawood on the east.

Woolworth's opened its new variety store on Nichols Road on the County Club Plaza in 1958, quadrupling the space it had occupied for two decades in its earlier location a block east. When this store opened, F.W. Woolworth Co. had 2,100 stores nationwide. Until 1978, the building adjoining the new Woolworth's housed a bowling alley that opened in 1940. As plans were laid for a general upscaling of the area in 1980, the J.C. Nichols Co. told Woolworth's that its lease would not be renewed. The news was the same for an adjacent multiscreen motion-picture theater, a cocktail lounge and a pasta parlor.

Saks Fifth Avenue, a national high-fashion retailer, moved into this new structure in 1982.

OVERLAND PARK
EARLY 1980s

Four-laned, divided streets were in place, but only a few new buildings dotted the landscape in the area between College Boulevard and Interstate 435. In the early 1980s this area was beginning to heat up as a real estate and construction bonanza. This photograph was taken from the roof of Yellow Freight's high-rise on Roe Boulevard, and looked west and southwest.

One Hundred Tenth Street curved toward Nall, where United Telephone was occupying a high-rise opened a few years before. Silhouetted on the hill in the distance, slightly left of center, was a Black & Veatch engineering building that opened at 112th and Lamar in 1976.

OVERLAND PARK
2 0 0 3

Although the patch of land in the foreground remains partly undeveloped, the last two decades have seen much of the rest of the area along College Boulevard and Interstate 435 fill in with two-, three-, and four-story office buildings, and hotels. Among the latter is the Sheraton, which towers over the Overland Park Convention Center in the distance. On the horizon to the left rises the tower on the new campus of Sprint, successor to United Telephone. On the horizon to the right, cranes signal more construction. Easy access, relatively inexpensive land and proximity to new residential neighborhoods made College Boulevard the area's fastest-growing commercial office district for years.

Fascinating as it is to react to how things once were, wouldn't it be doubly fascinating to know how some of the people in the *Then* photographs would react to our world today?

Those two horseback riders on Main Street in 1868 — on Page 4 — they might have dreamed that a great city would grow there. But would they have imagined what took place by the middle of the 20th century? Would they have thought skyscrapers would rise blocks to the south and crowds of commuters fill highways into and out of downtown? Could they have begun to speculate that, by the opening of the 21st century, skyscrapers would be rising and commuters jamming roads, not a few blocks away but many miles away, across county lines and state lines — in faraway places that were now considered part of a metropolis called "Kansas City"?

Those guests of Milton McGee's on the hillside south of downtown — see Page 12 — could they have thought that streets would carve up the land where they were sitting, and that commerce would then march away and leave much of that behind, and that by the 21st century voices would clamor to bring the area back to life? In their wildest dreams, could they have understood that people would want to build a temple to the performing arts near that same hillside?

In fact, the answer may well be "Yes" to each of these. The people in the *Then* pictures surely did not think they were living in a time or a place that was quaint, romantic or idyllic. That was simply their world, a thing to be navigated and survived. Not until decades after the fact do generations idealize the past. Instead, those 19th century human beings, like every generation since, probably presumed that the world of the future would be somehow sleeker, easier, more exalted — better.

There is much to value about times past. For instance, there is the shared experience provided by a compact downtown with busy streetscapes, which we mostly miss today. Nevertheless, those of us who walk the same ground today are realizing the dream of previous generations.

We live longer. More of us accomplish more things. We tolerate one another better.

And unlike our predecessors, we have learned that we have the opportunity to enhance the physical world around us — whether it means building things new, preserving things old, or sometimes simply leaving nature alone.

Above: new reflecting pool, Nelson-Atkins Museum of Art.

Facing page: West on 12th from Main Street.

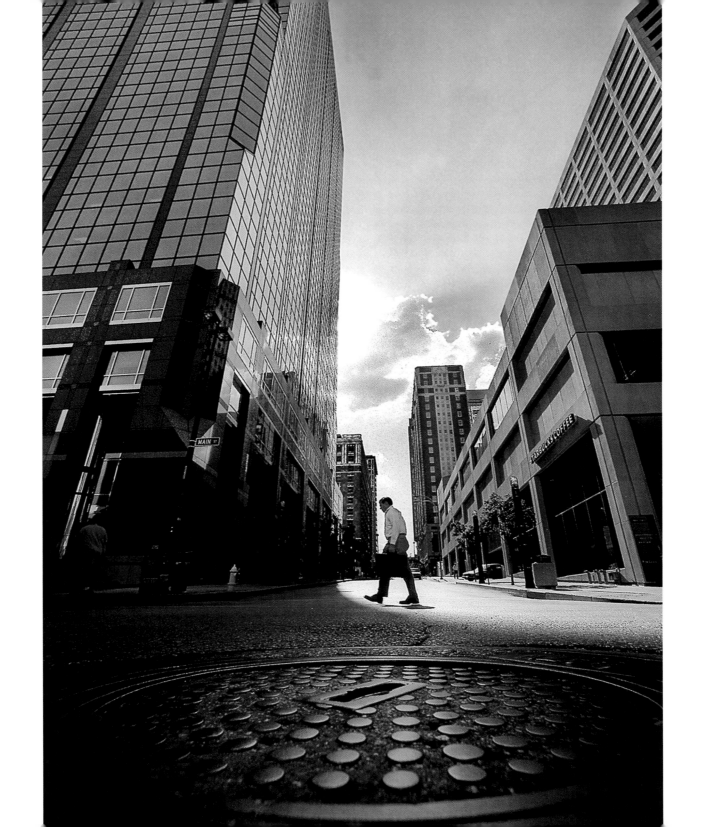

ACKNOWLEDGMENTS

As with the first volume of *Kansas City Then & Now*, the friendliness and helpfulness of Kansas Citians made this book possible. From professional archivists and librarians, to expert amateur volunteers, to those who came forward with rare photos, to those who opened their businesses or properties for new photos to be made — all gave information, images or insights that would have been otherwise impractical or impossible to obtain.

At the Special Collections Department of the Kansas City Public Library, director Mary Beveridge, Daniel Coleman and Sara Nyman and the rest of the staff proved unfailingly helpful on this as on many previous projects.

The same is true of David Boutros and his staff at the Western Historical Manuscript Collection-Kansas City.

Also of great help:

■ The Jackson County Historical Society and David Jackson, who pointed the way to some wonderful *Then* ideas.

■ At the Johnson County Museums, Collections Manager Kathy Daniels and before her Theresa Gonzalez.

■ The Wyandotte County Historical Society, headed by Executive Director Trish Schurkamp. Joel Thornton had numerous suggestions and dug up several fine images.

■ F.W. Wagner and his colleagues at the Overland Park Historical Society. They have assembled an interesting collection of photographs from that city's history.

■ Berryl Hennigh, who guided the way through the fine collection of photos held by the Lenexa Historical Society and housed at the Legler Barn Museum in Lenexa.

■ At the Clay County Archives and Historical Library, Kevin Fisher, who helped not only uncover several interesting images but also explained their context.

■ The historical photograph collection and other helpful materials in the Kansas Room of the Olathe Public Library.

■ Excelsior Springs Historical Museum.

Also thanks to Larry Hancks of the City of Kansas City, Kan.; Stuart Hinds of the Johnson County Library; Robert Ray and Teresa Gipson of the Special Collections Department, Miller Nichols Library at the University of Missouri-Kansas City; Norma Haggerty of Kansas City, Barbara Andersen of Shawnee, and *The Star*'s editorial imaging department.

As for *Now* photos, many would not have been possible without the permission granted by the staff of various companies and agencies. Among them: Michael Roper, assistant manager of the Charles B. Wheeler Downtown Airport; John Clock and Gail Koenke of New Quality Hill; Mark Bruce at Kansas City Cold Storage; Darin Botelho and Joe Papst of Highwoods Properties, Terry Dell, Tom Paterka and Gary Roberg of Yellow Corp.; Brian Hedrick of Dean Realty Co.; employees and residents of the Sophian Plaza; and Sgt. Corey Rogers of City Hall security.

BIBLIOGRAPHY

BOOKS

■ Dory DeAngelo and Jane Fifield Flynn. *Kansas City Style: A Social and Cultural History of Kansas City as Seen Through Its Lost Architecture.* Kansas City: Fifield Publishing Co., 1992.

■ Janice Lee, David Boutros, Charlotte R. White and Deon Wolfenbarger. *A Legacy of Design: An Historical Survey of the Kansas City, Missouri, Parks and Boulevards System, 1893-1940.* Kansas City: Kansas City Center for Design Education and Research, in cooperation with the Western Historical Manuscript Collection-Kansas City, 1995.

■ Rick Montgomery and Shirl Kasper. *Kansas City: An American Story.* Kansas City: Kansas City Star Books, 1999.

■ James L. Soward. *Hospital Hill: An Illustrated Account of Public Healthcare Institutions in Kansas City, Missouri.* Kansas City: Truman Medical Center Charitable Foundation, 1995.

■ Wilda Sandy and Larry K. Hancks, technical editor. *Stalking Louis Curtiss, Architect: A Portrait of the Man and his Work.* Ward Parkway Press: Kansas City, Missouri, 1991.

ARCHIVES AND COLLECTIONS

Library of *The Kansas City Star*.
Special Collections Department, Kansas City Public Library.
Jackson County Historical Society, Independence.
Johnson County Museums of History.
Clay County Archives & Library, Liberty.
Overland Park Historical Society.
Lenexa Historical Society, housed at the Legler Barn Museum, Lenexa.
Western Historical Manuscript Collection, University of Missouri-Kansas City.
Special Collections, Miller Nichols Library, University of Missouri-Kansas City.

PHOTOGRAPHY

Historical photographs are from the files of *The Kansas City Star*, except as noted here. Modern photographs are by Monroe Dodd of *The Star*.

SC/KCPL. Special Collections, Kansas City Public Library, Kansas City, Missouri.

Dustjacket. Front: Special Collections, Kansas City Public Library, Kansas City. Back: Top left, Western Historical Manuscript Collection-Kansas City.

Page vi. Photo courtesy of the Lenexa Historical Society, housed at the Legler Barn Museum, 14907 W. 87th St. Parkway, Lenexa, Kansas.

2-3. SC/KCPL.

4. Western Historical Manuscript Collection-Kansas City.

6. Western Historical Manuscript Collection-Kansas City.

8. Special Collections, Kansas City Public Library, Kansas City, Missouri.

10. Photographic Archives, Olathe Public Library.

12. SC/KCPL.

14. Top and bottom, Clay County Archives and Historical Library.

16. SC/KCPL.

18. SC/KCPL.

20. SC/KCPL.

22. Excelsior Springs Historical Museum.

24. SC/KCPL.

26. Johnson County Museums.

28. Western Historical Manuscript Collection-Kansas City.

30. SC/KCPL.

32, 33. Johnson County Museums.

36-37. Johnson County Museums.

38. SC/KCPL.

40. Wyandotte County Historical Society and Museum.

42. Johnson County Museums.

Above: Looking west on Kansas Street from the courthouse square in Liberty, 1920s. Below: The same scene in 2003.

46. Johnson County Museums.

48. SC/KCPL. .

56. SC/KCPL.

58. SC/KCPL.

60. Johnson County Museums.

62. Johnson County Museums.

66. Excelsior Springs Historical Museum.

68-69. Top: Photographic Archives, Olathe Public Library.

70-71. Top: Library of Congress Prints and Photographs Division.

72. Photo courtesy of the Lenexa Historical Society, housed at the Legler Barn Museum, 14907 W. 87th St. Parkway, Lenexa, Kansas.

76. Overland Park Historical Society.

78. SC/KCPL.

82. Western Historical Manuscript Collection-Kansas City.

84. Overland Park Historical Society.

86. Courtesy Norma Haggerty, Kansas City.

88. Kansas City, Kansas, Planning & Zoning.

92. Clay County Archives and Historical Library.

94-95. SC/KCPL.

96. Kansas Collection, Kenneth Spencer Research Library, University of Kansas Libraries.

106. SC/KCPL.

110. Johnson County Museums.

116. SC/KCPL.

118. Wyandotte County Historical Society and Museum.

122. SC/KCPL.

128. SC/KCPL.

130. Wyandotte County Historical Society and Museum.

132. Johnson County Museums, courtesy Barbara Andersen.

134. SC/KCPL.

138. SC/KCPL.

142, 144, 146, 148. Dick Millard Sr., photographer. Jackson County Historical Society Archives.

152. Clay County Archives and Historical Library.

162. Western Historical Manuscript Collection-Kansas City.

178. Jackson County Historical Society Archives.

180. Used by permission of the University of Missouri-Kansas City Libraries, Special Collections Department.

182. Bill Curtis, photographer. Johnson County Museums.

188. Jackson County Historical Society Archives.

190. Jackson County Historical Society Archives.

192. Jackson County Historical Society Archives.

196. Photo courtesy of the Lenexa Historical Society, housed at the Legler Barn Museum, 14907 W. 87th St. Parkway, Lenexa, Kansas.

198. SC/KCPL.

200. Overland Park Historical Society.

210. Bill Johns.

214. Jackson County Historical Society Archives.

216. Johnson County Museums.

218. Overland Park Historical Society.

234. Sun Publications, Sun Newspaper Photographs Collection, Johnson County Museums.

240. Aaron Showalter.

INDEX

A

Argentine 40, 41
Armour, Swift and Burlington Bridge (ASB) ....
....104, 105
Armourdale 41
AT&T Town Pavilion 137
Atkins, Mary 30
Auditorium Theater 52

B

Barry community (Missouri) 230
Bartle Hall 199
Bingham, George Caleb 44
Bingham-Waggoner Historical Society 45
bluffs ..6
Boley Building 136, 137
Broadway Bridge 206, 207
Brush Creek 80, 81, 126

C

Carver, George Washington 10
Central High School 184
Centropolis Hotel 56
Charles Evans Whittaker U.S. Courthouse....113, 179
City Center Square 103
City Market....................................5, 57, 192, 193
City Union Mission..107
Clay County, Missouri 14, 134, 152
Clay County Historical Museum 15, 153
Coates House...8
Coates Opera House 52
Coca-Cola building (later Western Auto building)......
....116, 117
Conser building 84, 85

Cosmopolitan Club 77
Country Club Plaza 126, 127, 228, 229, 236, 237
Crown Center shops 157
Curtiss, Louis 24, 80, 136

D

Dallas community (Missouri) 108
Delk, Edward Buehler 138
Donnelly, Father Bernard 54
Douglass Hospital 232, 233
DST Systems 29

E

East Bottoms 58
Eighth Street tunnel 28
Eighth Street viaduct................................162, 163
Electric Park 58, 59
Elms Hotel 22, 23, 66, 67
Emery, Bird, Thayer......................................164
Excelsior Springs 22, 23, 66, 67

F

Fairway, Kansas 43
F.W. Woolworth Co. 236
First Baptist Church 48, 49
First National Bank 9

G

Gardner, Kansas 62, 63
Gillham, Robert 16
Gillis House...56
Giralda Tower 228, 229
Grain Valley..142, 143
Gunn, Frederick 24

H

Hagaman, Frank 60
Hall Brothers 156
Hallmark 157
Harzfeld's Womens Wear.................................164
Heart of America Bridge 105
Heart of America United Way............................25
Heim, Ferdinand 128
Hill, Frederick 125
Hotel Continental 91
Hotel Kansas Citian......................................91
Hotel Lyndon...172
Huron Building 176, 177

I

Independence, Missouri 44, 45

J

J.C. Nichols Co. 236
Jackson County, Missouri 140-143, 144, 146, 148
Jackson County Home 146
John Taylor Dry Goods Co. 86, 170
Johnson County Industrial Airport.....................169
Johnson County, Kansas ..32, 73, 132, 196, 216, 219,
   234
Johnson, Rev. Thomas 42
Jones Store 172, 173, 208, 209

K

Kansas City Athletic Club.................................91
Kansas City Bank & Trust Co. 223
Kansas City Cold Storage building 105
Kansas City Junior College.........................184, 185
Kansas City Marriott Country Club Plaza hotel....195

INDEX

Kansas City Public Library 120
Kansas City Southern Industries Inc. 31
Kansas City, Kansas ....
    41, 47, 64, 88, 89, 119, 131, 176, 177, 232, 233
Kansas State Historical Society. 43
Katz Drug Co. 136
Kauffman Legacy Park 101
KCMO television....................................204, 205
Kemper Arena 79
Kessler, George 154
Kump, Frank Hubbard 128

L

Lackman, William 32, 34
Last Chance.......................................186, 187
Leawood, Kansas 235
Legler, Edwin A. 72
Lenexa, Kansas 34, 72, 73, 110, 111
Lenexa Historical Society 72
Liberty, Missouri 14, 92, 93, 152, 153
Liberty Memorial.............................166, 167
Lincoln Academy 39
Linwood Shopping Center 175
Little Blue community (Missouri) 148

M

Mark Twain Tower 91
Martin City, Missouri 144, 145
McClure flats.......................................82, 83
McGee's addition 12
McGee, Elijah Milton 12
Menorah Hospital 101
Merriam, Kansas 183
Metropolitan Street Railway 28

Mill Creek viaduct................................139
Muehlebach Brewery............................212
Muehlebach Hotel 49

N

Nelson, William Rockhill 80, 100
New Century AirCenter 63, 169
Newman Theater 102
North Kansas City, Missouri 224, 225

O

Oak Park Shopping Center 197
Olathe, Kansas ....
    10, 11, 68
Olathe Naval Air Station 168
Our Lady of Perpetual Hope 54
Overland Park, Kansas................76, 84, 85, 132, 133,
197, 200, 201, 219, 235, 238, 239
Overland Park Convention Center 239
Overland Park State Bank 76, 77
Ozark National Life................................121

P

Parallel Parkway 119
Paseo Bridge 202, 203
Penn Valley Park................................154, 155, 156
Pennsylvania Avenue 124, 125
Pershing Road 116, 117
Petticoat Lane 86, 164, 165
Pflumm Road 72, 73
Philadelphia Baptist Church 183
Platte County, Missouri.........................230
Polytechnic Institute 184

Q

Quality Hill 16, 18, 25, 28, 30, 198
Quindaro 232
Quinlan Place 50
Quinlan, C.C. 50

R

Redemptorist Monastery 54
Redemptorist Our Lady of Perpetual Hope 55
Results of County Planning 141
Rockhill Tennis Club.............................101
Rosedale, Kansas 46, 47

S

Saks Fifth Avenue 237
San Dora Hotel 122
Santa Fe Place Apartments 157
Shawnee, Kansas........................26, 27, 216, 217
Shawnee Indian Mission 42
South Park community (Kansas) 182, 183
St. Joseph Hospital 174, 175
Stover, Russell 102
Stowers Institute for Medical Research................101
Strang, William 76
Streets, roads and highways
    10th street 8, 9
    11th street.....................86, 87, 164, 184, 185
    12th street......................208, 209, 226, 227
    13th Street......................................198, 199
    16th Street.......................................12
    18th Street....................................212, 213
    20th Street......................................83
    31st Street....................................204, 205
    95th Street.....................................218

INDEX

Askew Street 60, 61
Baltimore Avenue 13, 48, 49, 90, 91
Barry Road...231
Broadway...28, 122, 123
Brookside Boulevard 158, 159
College Boulevard 238
Emanuel Cleaver II Boulevard 101
Grand Avenue...........................56, 57, 82, 180, 222
Grand Boulevard 181, 223
Highland Avenue...50, 51
Holmes Road...144, 145
Hunter Avenue 54
Interstate 29 203
Interstate 35 ....19, 189, 203
Interstate 435 ....109, 238
Interstate 70 215
J.C. Nichols Parkway 139
Jefferson Street 18, 19
Kansas City Road 32, 110
Kansas Highway 10..216
Kersey Coates Drive 78, 79
Lee's Summit Road 147
Linwood Boulevard..........................55, 174, 175
Little Blue Road...149
Locust Street 120, 121
Main Street 4, 5, 102, 103, 114, 115, 156,
157, 170, 192, 193, 194, 195
McClure's Court 82
McGee Street 82
Metcalf Avenue 77, 218, 219
Mill Creek Parkway 74, 138
Mission Road..42
Montgall Avenue 58, 59
Nall Avenue...234
Ninth Street 16, 52, 53, 112, 113
Parallel Parkway 119
Pennsylvania Avenue 124, 125
Pershing Road...116, 117
Petticoat Lane 86, 164, 165

Pflumm Road 72, 73
Quivira Road...196
Rockhill Road..80, 81
Santa Fe Trail Drive..111
Second Street 6
Sixth Street Expressway 214
Southwest Boulevard 46, 47, 186, 187
Southwest Trafficway 188
Troost Avenue 106, 107, 172, 173
U.S. 40 — Victory Highway 118
U.S. 69 132
Vine Street 226
Walnut Street 136, 137
Washington Street...........................24, 25, 30, 31
Westport Road..150, 151
Winn Road 135
Wornall Road 108, 109
Wyandotte Street...128, 129
Warner Plaza 114, 115

Studio Building 112, 113

T

12th Street Viaduct 79
Telephone building 87
Temple B'nai Jehudah 86
Thayer Building..16, 17
The Kansas City Star 82
theaters 90
Theis. Frank A. 101
Thompson, Frank 34
Tomahawk Creek...132
Tower Plaza Shopping Center 131
Traders Bank Building...222
Traders on Grand 223
Trans World Airlines (TWA)..................212, 213
Troost Park 38, 39
Truman, Harry S. 141, 146

Truman Medical Center East 147

U

Union Station 190, 191
University of Kansas City 101

V

Virginia Dare store 164
Virginia Hotel 24
Voight Building 84, 85
Volker, William 7

W

Waggoner, William 44
Waldo 210, 211
Walker Elementary 182
Warder Grand Opera House ....
....see Auditorium Theater
Washington Hotel 30
Washington Square Park.............................116, 117
Waterway Park 88
Webster School 129
West Bottoms 78
West Side 188, 189
West Terrace Park 78, 79
Western Auto building 117
Westport, Missouri 74, 75, 124, 150, 151
Westport City Hall 125
William Volker fountain 101
Winnwood Lake 134
Wish-Bone Restaurant..................................194, 195
Wood, Willis 90, 91
Wyandotte County, Kansas 65, 118, 130